MW01054236

The PBS Companion

The PBS Companion

A History of
Public Television

David Stewart

New York

Publisher's Cataloging-in-Publication Data
Stewart, David (David C.), 1927–
    The PBS companion : a history of public television / David Stewart. — 1st ed.
    p. cm.
    ISBN: 1-57500-050-4
    1. Public Broadcasting Service (U.S.) 2. Public television—United States.
  I. Title.
    HE8700.79.U6S74 1999   384.55'4'0973
                                        QBI99-720

The publisher has made every effort to secure permission to reproduce copyrighted material and would like to apologize should there have been any errors or omissions.

TV Books, L.L.C.
1619 Broadway, Ninth Floor
New York, NY 10019
www.tvbooks.com

Interior design by Rachel Reiss.
Manufactured in the United States of America.

Contents

For my children and grandchildren.

Acknowledgments

Many people have assisted me by supplying reference material: public TV station personnel; Tom Conners, director of the Public Broadcasting Archive at the University of Maryland; and personal friends. I am indebted to Michael Ambrosino and Robert Davidson for allowing me to use portions of their lengthy interviews with, respectively, David Fanning and Joan Cooney. Oui Wong typed the manuscript with skill and patience. Special thanks to Steve Behrens, editor of *Current Newspaper* where these chapters first appeared, for his unfailing encouragement and keen editorial judgment.

Introduction

In some respects writing this book has been an indulgence, an opportunity to recall the beginnings of some major public television programs that have given much pleasure to millions. It did not occur to me until I had completed several of the chapters that collectively they might represent an informal history of public television.

It has been necessary in these pages to make occasional references to noncommercial television's unique, somewhat arcane, structure. But those who are anxious to learn more about its complex institutional development will need to look elsewhere. This book is about programs and the people who created them.

Noncommercial television has occupied a part of America's cultural landscape for nearly fifty years. It first appeared as "educational TV," assuming its "public" name in 1967. It is a tribute to the best programs and their producers that the genre has survived so many distractions: real and imagined government and corporate influence, intense rivalries between institutions within its fragile web, its own administrative ineptness, frequent bouts of banality, and politicians who cannot resist grandstanding, to name a few. Many will wish to add its unremitting on-air pleas for financial support.

Critics have been generally kind to public television programming, perhaps too kind, often citing inadequate funds as the chief reason for a poor program rather than a producer's lack of imagination or insufficient grasp of the subject. In addition to a handful of professional observers with a gift for graceful incisiveness—Tom Shales, David Denby,

Robert Coles, John O'Conner, Richard Schickle, Pauline Kael, and Frank Getlein come to mind—there are hundreds who seem intent upon trivializing the outpouring of a medium that frequently fosters superficiality without anyone's assistance. Public television needs the work of more intelligent critics as much as it needs more money.

Production of serious drama and sophisticated comedy seems beyond public television's reach, as do programs that might be described as venturesome or experimental. The conventional explanation is that such programs require huge financial resources. The system produces excellent documentaries in very large numbers, but few programs characterized by wit, elegance, hilarity, or what in other times and places has been known as "dash" (a combination of stylishness and flair). Some would say that this is the result of intimidation by politicians and professional critics who misunderstand and misuse the word "elitism," swinging it with wild abandon like a blunt instrument in a crowded elevator.

I am unconvinced by the lack-of-money explanation and the we-must-not-appear-to-be-elite argument. I am more inclined to believe that public TV programs simply reflect the social, economic, and intellectual interests of those who are professionally associated with public broadcasting: the staffs of local stations, PBS, and regional organizations as well as those responsible for large-scale program financing. They are relatively conservative, reasonably well-educated people who seem quite comfortable with serious documentaries, mainstream music and dance performances, an earnest nightly news service, and programs to improve their cooking, homes, and gardens in addition to unusually inventive children's fare. The programming tastes of public TV professionals probably differ little from those of their audience. "Uncharacteristic" programs (e.g., *Brideshead Revisited* and *Upstairs, Downstairs*) are usually purchased, often from British sources. In more than forty years I have known dozens of program executives who thought that *Fawlty Towers* was hilarious, but not one of them would have considered producing anything similar.

Many would tell you that "safe" program production choices are made because "public TV can no longer afford to fail" (as if it once possessed this good fortune). Risks have occasionally been taken, often with re-warding results, as with *The Great American Dream Machine, An American Family,* and some single programs in the *P.O.V.* (point of view) series. In the main, however, public television audiences expect consistent, solid achievement—*Great Performances, American Masters,* Mark Russell's po-litical satire, *The Civil War*—and receive it from like-minded producers.

I once asked the head of BBC's TV programming what he looked for in a good producer. Without hesitation he replied, "A combination of an Oxford don and a fighter pilot." In my experience, people who have made the best programs are highly intelligent and seem to know a lot about many different things. They are "creative," of course, and good or-ganizers. More importantly they are persistent. Julia Child has great charm and culinary technique, Fred Rogers has a mission, Fred Wise-man is a uniquely gifted documentarian, but however different they may be, these and the other program makers described in this book share at least one characteristic: strong determination.

Making TV programs is a labor-intensive process and the product is usually ephemeral. Those who have created a substantial work, an *oeuvre,* in this medium possess an abundance of talent and a dedication to the long haul. Because of their desire to make a lasting mark upon such an impermanent medium, the influence of their accomplishments is out of all proportion to their numbers. Collectively they have added an important dimension to our cultural lives. What I have written is an attempt to celebrate their achievement.

Finally, a caveat. As might be expected, the history of public televi-sion programming has not been a seamless procession of one notable se-ries giving rise to another. The progression has been far more disorderly, not unlike the sequence of programs described in this book. Each chap-ter was created to stand alone, written for those who might benefit from contextual reminders. I hope that where overlaps occur they may serve to clarify the chronicle.

The Shakespeare Experience

When he died in 1982 many were astonished: Frank Baxter still alive in the 1980s! Many remembered him as mature, if not quite elderly, nearly thirty years before when he grasped national attention simply by talking to a TV camera about Shakespeare's plays and poetry.

In the early 1950s he was a curiosity, a professor on television, a bald, bespectacled, moonfaced man who lectured on Shakespeare in the same style he used in the classroom; as a reporter remarked, "without benefit of giveaways, girls, or gimmicks." What's more, to everyone's surprise—except perhaps that of his classroom students at the University of Southern California (USC)—he became an overnight sensation, first in Los Angeles, then throughout the country. He represented the kind of intellect to which millions aspired: disciplined and knowledgeable but self-effacing.

Frank Baxter's appearance coincided with the dawn of public television. In retrospect his popularity was extraordinarily fortuitous because it helped a large national audience to consider TV as more than a conveyor belt for commercial entertainment.

Alhough his early programs were aired on commercial TV, along with NBC's *Omnibus* and Leonard Bernstein's music lectures, Baxter became extremely useful to the educational TV stations that were just getting on their feet in the mid-1950s. "Like Frank Baxter" was a phrase often used by producers of noncommercial programs.

When Baxter came to television in 1953, he was in his late fifties and had been a skillful and experienced lecturer at USC for twenty-three years, named one of America's most popular teachers in a national student poll. KNXT, the CBS station in Los Angeles, offered the University an hour of "public service time" each week at 11 A.M. on Saturdays.

Although he complained that he would be talking to an audience of three—"two retired librarians and a bedridden man"—Baxter was delighted. As it happens, about 400,000 watched him on TV, 350 paid twelve dollars to take English 356a for credit, and another 900 audited the class. CBS, bemused but not unaware of Baxter's potential, recorded the programs on kinescope and made plans to broadcast them nationally. Three *Shakespeare on TV* series were produced in 1953.

In December Baxter flew to New York where, along with Rod Serling, Mary Martin, Jerome Robbins, and the producers of *Omnibus,* he received the prestigious Sylvania Award. A few months later he found himself in the Los Angeles Palladium, standing on stage amid Donald O'Connor, Eve Arden, and Lucille Ball and Desi Arnaz. Looking amused and conspicuous in his conservative suit and tie, he held a 1953 Los Angeles–area Emmy in each hand—one for "most outstanding male performer," the other for "best public affairs program."

Asked to say a few words, Baxter said, "I'm sorry to announce that the person who deserves this award—William Shakespeare—cannot be here, due to a long absence. I would, however, like to thank my writer, who, by a strange coincidence, is also named William Shakespeare." The audience roared. As John Freeman wrote in the *San Diego Union,* "It was inconceivable . . . and quite wonderful." Dr. Frank C. Baxter had stolen the show. He was, unbelievably, a star.

Francis Condie Baxter was born in 1896 in Newbold, New Jersey. He went to work when he was eight, serving glasses of water to patrons in the box seats of Philadelphia's Civic Opera House. He dropped out of high school after one year and became an office boy in a chemical plant, eventually becoming the firm's bookkeeper.

After a year in the Army Medical Corps during the final year of World War I, Baxter was admitted to the University of Pennsylvania where, by

1928, he had financed himself with scholarships and university jobs through undergraduate and master's degrees. A frustrated actor in college plays, he later complained that he was always cast as "a lawyer or doctor or in some nonconsequential role." He seems to have been more successful as a radio announcer ("I read everything: recipes, the weather,... advice to the lovelorn") on Philadelphia's WOO.

Shortly before departing for England and Cambridge University in 1928, he married Lydia Morris, who had been his student at the University of Pennsylvania. The newlyweds were accompanied by Baxter's exceptionally domineering mother.

"My father had a problem," says Baxter's daughter. "He couldn't do anything without his mother. When he was young and invited out he would ask the host if he could bring his mother. Eventually my mother presented him with an ultimatum; my father would need to choose between them. My grandmother moved out. When we went to California, she lived near us but separately. She and my mother never spoke. My father used to take my brother and me to see her each Sunday."

Baxter completed his Cambridge doctorate in English literature in 1932, two years after he had begun teaching at USC.

The Emmy awards in 1954 was an important marker in Baxter's life. In the years ahead he would win five more Emmys and enough honors and citations to crowd the home in South Pasadena where he lived with his wife, two children, several thousand books, a Globe Theatre model he had made to illustrate his lectures, and several models of early printing presses he had also constructed.

Baxter had few misgivings about his association with commercial TV, contending that it held great promise for academic programs. "Looking at it from a cold-blooded standpoint," he observed in 1954, "I feel there is a real market for this kind of program. It appeals to a large middle class ... that could be valuable to an advertiser. ... The mail we get is from solid citizens. Their letters are literate; the sentences have verbs in them."

After completing three fifteen-program Shakespeare series, he embarked upon a strenuous schedule of new TV productions and speaking engagements that was the envy of many in show business and the occasional dismay of his academic colleagues. Some teachers felt he had "sold out" and dubbed him "the Liberace of the library."

"I have to watch myself with my colleagues," he wrote in a letter during this period. "Talking about my sundry adventures in darkest Hollywood must be infuriating and something of a bore to them."

Throughout his most active television production years Baxter continued to teach four courses at USC, serving for eight years as chairman of the English Department. Upon retirement he noted that he had missed only three or four of his regular classes despite the demands of his television career. Though he said that his crowded schedule was "hell on wheels," he was clearly enjoying himself.

In 1954 Baxter threw himself into another and longer TV series, *Now and Then,* in which he talked about a broad range of literary interests from Egyptian hymns to Edwin Arlington Robinson. It was broadcast on ninety-five stations of the CBS network. This was followed by *Rennaissance on TV,* again for CBS, and the first of three series called *Harvest* for the NBC network. *Harvest* was designed to express "man's achievements in art, literature, public affairs, and science."

Harvest, a total of eighty-four half-hours, offered Baxter an opportunity to indulge a wide variety of his considerable interests: the Civil War, Elizabethan naval battles, the *McGuffey Reader,* the history of the Red Cross, Altamira cave drawings, and American clipper ships. Nearly all the programs were illustrated by charts, photographs, and paintings from his personal collection as well as models he had made himself. (His Shakespeare TV lectures had been animated by wooden figures of actors from the over three hundred he had carved.)

Writing to Robert Hudson at the National Educational TV and Radio Center in Ann Arbor, Michigan, Baxter explained, "*Harvest* for NBC [is] very much like the CBS *Now and Then,* save that NBC is giving me expensive and imaginative production beyond my wildest dreams."

The expense was only relative to his first austere studio arrangement—Baxter behind a lectern. CBS's seventeen-page contract for eighteen *Renaissance* programs provided that the network pay USC one

hundred dollars a week for the services of Baxter and any other professors working on the production. Subject to a separate contract, CBS
gave the Educational TV Center in Ann Arbor copies of the programs to
distribute to noncommercial stations.

Baxter's fame rested in part upon his ability as a talker, someone who
could explain how an early printing press or a sonnet worked. He had
an exceptionally retentive memory and uncommonly broad interests.
But the touchstone of his success was his intellectual energy, the enthusiasm he brought to his subjects.

By 1954, with CBS broadcasting the Shakespeare series and *Now and
Then* "coast-to-coast," Baxter, if not yet a hot property, was rapidly gaining national recognition. TV columnists welcomed but were puzzled by
his growing popularity alongside wrestling events and sitcoms.

"How odd for a lecturer on literature to have not one but two television shows!" wrote Val Adams in *The New York Times*. "Dr. Baxter has
emerged as TV's first intellectual glamour boy.... The professor's new
program shatters forever the theory that television programs must have
movement. The only movement in Dr. Baxter's program is that of his
lips.... Without interruption he stands alone talking into the camera.
And he seems to enjoy it."

Baxter starred in a new series of science specials sponsored by the
Bell System, including "Our Mr. Sun," produced and directed by Hollywood's well known Frank Capra (*Mr. Deeds Goes to Town* and *Lost Horizon,* among many other popular movies). As in the other science
specials, Baxter was cast as "Dr. Research," teamed with Eddie Albert as
a writer who is after the sun's story. Together they investigate the sun's
role in people's lives, sometimes appearing with cartoon characters (a
technical innovation at the time) such as "Chloro Phyll." Other Bell programs explained blood ("Hemo the Magnificent"), genetics ("The
Thread of Life"), and cosmic rays ("The Strange Case of Cosmic Rays").
Warner Brothers picked up the genre, producing four more programs,
all featuring Baxter, including one on relativity, "About Time." As stiff
and earnest as some of these programs may seem today, they remained
extraordinarily durable and videocassettes are still available today.

○ ○ ○

Baxter inevitably had to manage some problems of celebrity. In a 1956 letter to Elise Schiller he writes: "There are some stores I can no longer patronize for I seem to have . . . a reception whenever I stand still."

Though he enjoyed some of the attention, Baxter was an intensely private person. "I love mankind but find people very trying," he revealed in response to Ms. Schiller's questions.

Lydia, his daughter (named after his wife), remarked later, "He didn't have friends, was never gregarious. My mother said he could be very fond of people, but if they asked something of him it would turn him off. "He could be very quiet and moody for long periods of time. He couldn't stand moodiness in others, but he seemed unaware of his own silences."

Though Baxter's rise to a unique sort of TV fame solved many financial problems that had plagued him for years, it seems not to have resolved a variety of difficulties for his wife and children.

"I got out early," said his son, Frank Jr., who dropped out of USC and joined the Army. "My father was the sort of fellow it was difficult to compete with. Also, since he never had a childhood himself, he couldn't understand his own children. When we were three and four and did something improper he would say to us with disgust, 'Now that was really childish.'"

Baxter's daughter Lydia didn't get along well with him until she had grown up. "He couldn't stand immaturity," she recalled. "Mother, realizing this, tried to keep us from him. We were fed in our own rooms until we were eight or nine."

Ken Harwood, one of Baxter's USC students and later a professor himself, has commented, "It is a task, a chore, and a burden to be the offspring of an academic, because you have so much to, quote, live up to, unquote."

Soon after winning his first two Emmys, Lucille Ball invited Baxter to make a guest appearance on *I Love Lucy,* but he declined. "I love lucidity," he commented prissily.

He did, however, become a full-fledged personality of the TV age—plain-spoken, not without humor, and decidedly avuncular. He appeared frequently on network TV, less often in the role as lecturer in his own fields of expertise than as the personality who embodied erudition for the television audience. Baxter appeared on *The Telephone Hour, Playhouse 90,* and dozens of other programs. In the late 1950s, he was host for *Telephone Time,* dramatizations of true stories featuring well-known Hollywood actors.

The TV personality stomped up and down the land talking to Rotarians ("Businessmen and Books"), lawyers ("Mass Education and the Complacent American"), and public relations executives ("Deliver us from the hard sell and the pretty packaged lie"). He advised a gathering of Mobil Oil dealers in Las Vegas that "nothing takes the place of consistent and varied reading."

Baxter occasionally took on pretenders to Shakespeare's authorship ("Baxter Scoffs at Marlowe" was a common newspaper line), but his arguments were conventional, attracting little academic interest. For all of his insistence on academic rigor, it was his enthusiasm and assertive TV style that commanded attention.

Before the end of the decade Baxter was engaged to write and preside over a series of fifteen half-hour programs, *The Written Word,* filmed at USC for the National Educational TV and Radio Center. In substance the programs were drawn from his USC course "History of Books and Printing." On one program he made papyrus and wrote on it, on another he devised a language of his own from symbols.

The series formally united commercial television's foremost intellectual with educational TV, the forerunner of public TV. Later, when National Educational Television (NET) took up residence in New York, Baxter was hired to host a Shakespeare drama series, *An Age of Kings,* that NET had purchased from the BBC. It was NET's first genuine success. There were then sixty noncommercial stations on the air, and Baxter found himself becoming closely identified with programs carried by the new system.

The educational programs "act as the touchstone and standard by which commercial public service programming is judged," he told the *New York Herald-Tribune,* though he warned that "TV is no vending machine for education." Baxter seldom played the apologist: "At its worst TV... appeals to the eight-year-old intelligence and the six-year-old intellect," he said.

Three years later NET invited Baxter to return to host a series of international documentaries, *Intertel,* a collaboration with Westinghouse. His first program in the series was "The Quiet War," about Vietnam.

If Frank Baxter had continued to concentrate upon teaching Shakespeare on TV, his work would have been an interesting but isolated cultural event. It was the broad range of his interests and his ability to share them with large audiences that made him attractive and drew attention to the real possibilities of teaching by television.

From 1954 on the awards and honors rolled in: a Peabody award in 1956, Toastmasters International's first Golden Gavel. He was twice invited to read poetry and receive awards at the Library of Congress. Brandeis honored him "for reawakening interest in the classroom." USC and three colleges gave him honorary degrees.

One morning in May 1961 the *Los Angeles Times* dispatched a reporter and photographer to record his last classroom appearance ("Dr. Frank Baxter Delivers Final Lecture at SC, Makes Sparks Fly"). The camera saw a tall man standing before fifty alert USC students, his body tilted slightly toward them, his arms and large hands outstretched, inviting, almost beseeching, their full attention. His last words from Shakespeare's *The Tempest:* "My charms are all o'er thrown...." And from himself, characteristically: "Take the next part of this course next semester. Or I shall haunt you."

Throughout his career, the USC public relations office tirelessly exploited Baxter's accomplishments through a snowstorm of press releases. He rivaled the University's football team in public relations value and in 1964, despite his aversion to spectator sports, he provided commentary on a special record celebrating that year's Trojan football season.

Here was an authentic scholar who had become famous, certainly ubiquitous, through his exposure on a still new and alluring medium. In many respects he was the press agent's dream: a familiar figure who was also the object of universal admiration. As Arthur Miller's Willy Loman might have observed, Baxter was not only liked, he was well liked.

In later years Baxter hosted two Westinghouse-sponsored series—a travel and adventure program, *The Four Winds,* and then *The Fair Adventure,* sixty TV programs and thirty radio progams of Baxter reading from Shakespeare's plays and poetry. He chose the title from *King John* (Act 5, Scene 5): "The day shall not be up so soon as I, to try the fair adventure of tomorrow."

Public readings had long been something of a Baxter specialty. In 1965, as a professor emeritus, he became USC's official Reader in Residence, offering several afternoon poetry and prose readings on campus each spring and fall.

As Baxter grew older, he increasingly suffered problems relating to a diabetic condition diagnosed many years before. His mobility was restricted but he resolutely refused to exercise, to eat healthful food. He smoked his pipes and short black cigars; when he developed lip cancer, he responded by adjusting the position of the pipe stem in his mouth.

He read constantly. The man who had created hundreds of television programs and inspired thousands more could rarely be lured to watch a TV screen.

On the last evening of his life he enjoyed an elegant restaurant meal with his son and daughter-in-law. Later, as he did not look well, they took him, protesting, to the local hospital emergency ward where he joked and flirted with the nurses until the doctor arrived.

"Have you ever had heart problems?" asked the physician.

"Never," replied Baxter, and died. He was eighty-six.

Many of the obituaries referred to Baxter's acting aspirations. He had always wanted to be an actor, said a close friend, Aerol Arnold, who took over his Shakespeare classes when Baxter retired, "He was an old ham." Many recalled his classroom interpretations of Falstaff, Hotspur, and Prince Hal. Former students commented upon his career as a professor. But the words "TV personality" appear more often. It was a subtle shift, requiring years, a transformation Frank Baxter would have no doubt appreciated and approved. In the end, TV claimed him as one of its own.

An Age of Kings

It was public TV's first unqualified national success, a smash hit. Before *Masterpiece Theatre, American Playhouse,* or *Hollywood Television Theatre,* there was *An Age of Kings,* Shakespeare's history plays in fifteen parts, a chronicle of Britain's monarchs from Richard II (1399) to Richard III (1484).

"Easily one of the most magnificent efforts of the TV season," announced the *New York Herald-Tribune.* "It is one of the nicest things that has happened to TV in years."

The series began nationally October 20, 1961, to the intense pleasure of managers at the sixty noncommercial TV stations then on the air, who had begun to wonder whether they would ever be able to break away from their earnest, informative, but frequently mundane program image. *An Age of Kings* was not, however, a radical change of style. This was, after all, Shakespeare and, what's more, a serious British Broadcasting Corporation production. The National Educational Television and Radio Center (NETRC) that had purchased and was distributing the series was eager to emphasize its educational value, not its entertainment potential, referring to it as "an experience in historical and cultural understanding."

NETRC—then in Ann Arbor, Michigan, and soon to change its name to National Educational Television (NET) and move to New York—had plenty to crow about, but to brag in a conventional way risked a clash with the commercial television industry, which was still bridling over the government's reservation of channels for "noncommercial educational use" nearly ten years earlier. Restraining the natural impulse to boast about the series was frustrating; reviews in major news organizations were excellent and enticing. *Newsweek* said Shakespeare could [now be] considered box office, "especially when the Bard is run as a cliffhanger." "Whatever may be said of their ethics," wrote *The New York Times*, "those noblemen make for superb entertainment."

One element of *An Age of Kings* that received only faint attention at the time was in some respects its most important in the history of public broadcasting: it was the first nationally distributed noncommercial series to receive support from a commercial source, the Humble Oil and Refining Co. (marketer of Esso gasoline, later renamed Exxon).

Brice Howard, a well-known public TV producer and executive for NET, KERA, and KQED, bought the BBC's *An Age of Kings* for NETRC. It was the first of many acquisitions of British programs—dramas, documentaries, and light entertainment—that would define American noncommercial television programming for decades, generating both praise and scorn.

The BBC broadcast the series in 1960, the year it was sold to American educational television. That year it was also seen on commercial TV in New York and Washington, D.C., where public television had not yet been established.

An Age of Kings was a remarkable tour de force. Shakespeare's full history cycle had been produced in London's Old Vic Theatre between 1955 and 1960. Before that it had not been seen in its entirety since 1905, when all the plays had been produced in one week at Stratford-upon-Avon. BBC producer Peter Dewes assembled a small repertory company of fifteen actors, a group that was augmented as the scripts required. The leading roles were contracted out to more experienced actors, but not "stars." Stanley Morris designed a set that could be modified with projected images. Michael Hayes directed the plays, and original music was composed by Christopher Whelen.

Each of the programs was given a new TV title: thus the opener,

Richard II (acts 1, 2, and 3) became "The Hollow Crown," and was followed by *Richard II* (acts 3, 4, and 5), entitled "The Deposing of a King."

A montage of heraldic banners opened each episode. The production was swiftly paced and had an authentic look. The cast of *Henry V* had "pudding basin" haircuts that gave way to thick long manes in later programs. However hastily created, the filmed background projections worked wonderfully well. Images for the Battle of Shrewsbury were shot in a farmer's field, made grim by long black plumes from smokebombs. The Battle of Bosworth—which takes place in a bog—was staged in a studio where the set decorators had mixed mud, water, and peat in an area of just sixteen by twenty feet, but in the tightly shot Bosworth sequence, disbelief was quite adequately suspended.

In his *San Francisco Chronicle* review of the first program, Terence O'Flaherty remarked that "the series is performed by a group of young actors from the English stage." Frank Baxter, host of the series, refers to them as "provincial actors," saying that this explains their lack of mannered speech. Neither Baxter nor O'Flaherty could hardly have foreseen the fame that awaited some of those performers—the young Sean Connery, for example, who played Hotspur in the first four programs, or Judy Dench, who played Catherine, Princess of France.

One of the most appealing features of the series was the introductions and closing comments by Frank Baxter, a professor of English literature at the University of Southern California. A man of extraordinary energy, intelligence, and wit, Baxter had almost single-handedly created the concept of "educational television" with his earlier CBS series, *Shakespeare on TV.* An American graduate of Cambridge University, he had been teaching at USC since 1937. By the time he became host of *An Age of Kings,* his series *Harvest* (TV essays on a wide variety of subjects), *The Written Word* (a history of writing), and his series of Bell System–sponsored science specials had brought him a Peabody award, five Emmys, and national recognition. It was Baxter who had set the scene when Laurence Olivier's *Richard III* premiered on commercial television.

Throughout the run of *An Age of Kings,* NETRC publicity underlined the programs' uplifting values even as the audience reveled in the rip-

roaring dramas. "Insofar as we are able," one press release solemnly pro-
nounced, "cultural phenomena peculiar to the time and environment
will be ... explained, and significant themes will be explored wherever
appropriate." Baxter, the man chosen to straddle this education/enter-
tainment abyss, was an inspired choice. He was an instant hit.

NETRC announced that "Dr. Baxter will provide animated, informative, and far from pedantic commentary on the historical, geographical,
and genealogical backgrounds of the plays"—a considerably under-
stated description of the professor's theatrical proclivities. His comments, produced by Gerry Marans in the studios of KQED, San
Francisco, reminded many of their very best college teachers. Although
Baxter used diagrams, charts, and other "visual aids" (all of which he
created himself), it was his intellect, articulation, and prodigious memory that enthralled viewers. When he talked about the personalities and
relationships of the plays' principal characters, his descriptions included
the way Shakespeare saw them as well as how they were recorded by
history. His explanations of court traditions were as masterfully lucid as
his descriptions of costume details. He mesmerized his audiences and
became the darling of TV critics.

"When Warren Kraetzer and I met with the Humble Oil people in
Houston, they said, 'Wouldn't it be great if we could get Frank Baxter?'
We agreed immediately." This is the recollection of Nazaret ("Chick")
Cherkezian, interviewed in fall 1995, not long before he died of a brain
tumor at age seventy-two. He and Kraetzer were central to finding financial support for *An Age of Kings*. They convinced Humble Oil executives not only to buy national rights for the series but also to pay for
promotion and publicity. In our conversation, Cherkezian remembered
the rights costing about a quarter of a million dollars. This bargain was
possible in part because the BBC was eager to have its programs better
known in the U.S.

An Age of Kings, said Cherkezian, was "[public TV's] first big break-
through. It was the first money of this size outside the Ford Foundation grants. It probably totaled four hundred thousand dollars for the
series, the opening and closing segments production, and publicity.

The help for advertising was especially important. Before that time, we used to have about ten cents for promotion."

Cherkezian and Kraetzer, two native New Yorkers, met in 1949 at New York University (NYU), where they both worked in publicity and promotion. Together with a secretary they formed NYU's first department of television and began seeking opportunities to place their university professors ("from archaeology to zoology") on local TV stations, later producing their own programs with titles like *Our Living Heritage* and *The Bible as Literature.* NETRC eventually awarded them fifteen thousand dollars to produce a series on archaeology with time, staff, and facilities provided by WCBS. For a period in the early 1950s they were producing as many programs as the relatively young Boston station, WGBH. By 1959 Cherkezian and Kraetzer had been hired by NETRC and were assigned to the *Age of Kings* project. (Both remained in public TV, Cherkezian spending the last twelve years of his professional life [1974–86] organizing and directing the TV and radio activities of the Smithsonian Institution.)

Once the Humble Oil funding had been secured, thousands of posters were designed and distributed. A handsome publication describing the series was created and made available to local stations. "The American people cannot understand Shakespeare without somebody telling them what happened," said Cherkezian of the booklet. "All the names that came to the local stations requesting it were sent on to Humble Oil for marketing purposes." According to *Sponsor* magazine, "The response to the offering of an illustrated book is so tremendous that a first printing of one hundred thousand copies was exhausted one month after the announcement [of its availability]."

As for the programs themselves, Cherkezian remembered all the reviews as "marvelous." He recalled the series winning many awards for the best cultural programming, adding, "Of course, there was nothing else there except things produced by Jim Day at KQED, with equipment that made it seem like the cameras were shooting underwater. Everything about *An Age of Kings* was a first on a national scale. NET finally had something to promote throughout the country. It was our leader."

In his comprehensive history of public television in America, *The Vanishing Vision,* James Day describes *An Age of Kings* as "TV for the converted, designed for an audience already disposed to educational television's demanding fare. NET needed to . . . find a new audience whose appetites did not . . . tend toward the acquired tastes of high culture."

That was found, Day reminds us, in a Cripple Creek, Colorado, saloon where Max Morath pounded out rags on an upright piano. Jim Case, a producer at the new public TV station KRMA in Denver, converted Morath's music and patter into a series indisputably American and greatly entertaining. *The Ragtime Era* walked through a door to the nation's applause, a door that had been opened, somewhat improbably, by *An Age of Kings*.

That public television had its first national success with a British series was not lost on those in American noncommercial TV who had the greatest purchasing power. Before memories *of An Age of Kings* faded, *The Forsyte Saga,* a serial adaptation of John Galsworthy's novel, was imported and ran to great acclaim. Much later, an adaptation of Evelyn Waugh's *Brideshead Revisited,* likewise produced in England, became something of a cultural phenomenon. WGBH's *Masterpiece Theatre* provided a regular vehicle for drama imports, punctuated by lengthy, and extremely popular, serials such as *Upstairs, Downstairs* and *The Jewel in the Crown. Mystery!* created a space for (largely British) whodunits. And the importers did not overlook comedy; they made hits of *Monty Python's Flying Circus, Fawlty Towers, Are You Being Served?* and other Britcoms.

Some U.K. influence upon U.S. production substance and style was reflected in documentaries. *NOVA,* an American program invention, was based largely on the BBC's *Horizon* documentary series with which it subsequently shared programs. And the format of *Nature* was pioneered by such producers as Mick Rhodes and David Attenborough at the BBC's natural history unit in Bristol.

But it was the imported dramas that took a prominent place in the image of American public television, though they played a much smaller role in numbers of broadcast hours and had even less effect on American production style. Indeed, their influence on American productions was almost nonexistent. The most common explanation for the success of British drama is that BBC dramatic production budgets were large, and American public broadcasters could never muster that kind of support. Perhaps.

But a far likelier reason is the difference between British and American theatrical traditions—the environment in which actors, writers, producers, and directors work. Although such differences have narrowed, British theatrical professionals have more opportunity and inclination to move among the media. Alan Bennett, one of Britain's foremost writers, creates plays for stage, films, television, and radio. His *Talking Heads* series, well received when he adapted the plays for TV, was originally created for radio. He writes, acts, and directs in several media. Until recently, British writers have been offered remarkably broad opportunities in radio, a medium all but abandoned for drama in America since *Yours Truly, Johnny Dollar* left the air in 1962. A visitor to London is apt to encounter the same actors in daytime broadcasts who show up on stage that night in the West End. The profession resembles a large multimedia repertory company, and it has nurtured British theatrical talent throughout this century.

For many years a substantial number of Britain's most imaginative TV producers and writers have emerged from liberal arts colleges and universities, notably Oxford and Cambridge, where future program creators study history, math, literature, and philosophy, instead of "telecommunications" and other "practical" courses. This has added depth to subsequent opportunities for broad experience in the British entertainment industry.

When American public television seriously attempted costume drama (WGBH's *The Scarlet Letter* and WNET's *The Adams Chronicles* come to mind) the results were disappointing. And the idea of "humor-impaired" American public TV producing a comedy as hilarious as *Fawlty Towers* is, well, laughable.

In organizational style the BBC and American public TV continue to seem an ocean apart after nearly forty years of program sales and co-productions ("Our production," as the BBC used to say, "and your money").

During our 1995 conversation I asked Cherkezian (who had worked closely with the BBC for many years) if the "Beeb" had influenced U.S. public television, especially its program producers. "I used to believe it," he replied, "but I no longer do. We now seem to be saying, 'If the Brits can do it in six programs, we should be able to do it in nineteen.' I don't think we learned anything. The new breed running [U.S.] public TV thinks like commercial broadcasters. Few come out of the universities or the fine arts. A lot of them come out of broadcasting schools. They're into public TV hoping that as soon as they make their mark they can go into commercial broadcasting."

At the time when *An Age of Kings* was produced, program executives working for the BBC—then the only broadcaster in Britain and a recognized program force worldwide—could afford to be smug about their unique position. It was an attitude many did not deny and some fostered. Like Professor Higgins in Shaw's *Pygmalion,* a man who could not understand why women could not act more like men, BBC broadcasters were petulantly frustrated by the emerging public television service in America: a tax on radio and TV receivers was such a simple way to support public broadcasting, why didn't the Americans just do it? (Many Americans asked the same question.) For decades, U.S. public broadcasters working with their British counterparts were frequently exposed to exasperated and patronizing observations from British counterparts.

Some years ago I wrote to a number of British broadcasting executives and program producers, asking their assessment of public TV in America. I have lifted the following excerpt from a reply written by Roger Lawton, a man of wide broadcasting experience, then head of Meridian Television. It may stand for many of the opinions I received: "Good people in many areas, but far too many of them. And because of the funding issues, far too much time spent on simply keeping their stations above water."

Few of our British colleagues fully appreciate the strength of U.S. public TV's ties to its decentralized, educational roots. It was America's educators who led the fight for channels to be reserved for noncommercial use. And although NET and then PBS brought greater coherence to public TV's programming, local program judgments continue to dominate the system to a degree most foreign broadcasters find unimaginable.

But many of their well organized and handsomely supported national public TV systems have collapsed in the past decade, or have become *de facto* commercial operations when their governments decided they had grown too expensive.

In the same period, when some U.S. legislators spoke confidently about "zeroing out" public television, their political miscalculation swiftly became apparent: their constituents arrived in Washington to defend not CPB or PBS but *their local stations*. It seems doubtful that a more conventionally structured, centralized system could have mustered a similarly effective response.

Public TV's early "converted" audience has grown enormously since *An Age of Kings*. Most of its viewers moved on, gathering demographic strength, to additional costume dramas—lots of them—as well as *The Great American Dream Machine, The French Chef, NOVA,* and *The Civil War.* Children raised on *Sesame Street* eventually migrated to *Great Performances* and *Frontline.* Over a remarkably short time, these programs have created a special TV culture absorbed by America's wider cultural life.

Production standards have remained surprisingly high considering the uneven financial support. This is, I believe, the result of viewer expectations generated and nurtured by British programs. There were few attempts to copy them, thankfully. That would have been neither desirable nor possible. But for nearly four decades the strong British program presence in American public TV's national schedule has demonstrated excellence that invites audiences to watch the *next* program. In broadcast terms, this may be the most benign and effective influence that program producers in one country can exert on those in another.

The Ragtime Era

In the summer of 1959 an itinerant musician and sometimes TV producer, Max Morath, was playing piano for melodramas in the restored mining town of Cripple Creek, Colorado. A year later, the thirty-three-year-old graduate of Colorado College had written and performed a twelve-part TV series that would change noncommercial television forever.

Over the next five years—while the music rights were held by National Educational Television (NET)—*The Ragtime Era* became the most watched noncommercial series up to that time, run and rerun constantly by all the educational (and many commercial) stations throughout the country. The series and its more expansive fifteen-part sequel, *The Turn of the Century,* established Max Morath as a leading authority on ragtime as well as a popular performer.

It seems almost quaint to report that there was a time when public TV was uncertain whether it should seek to entertain or enlarge its audience. The problem in the late 1950s was how to take the first decisive step, to produce a popular series without compromising quality, to retain an educational message in an entertaining context.

The stations were at the brink of having a network. NET had arranged a Ford Foundation grant that purchased a videotape machine—then a very new device—for each of the fifty or so educational stations in the country. Soon thereafter, John F. "Jack" White, NET's energetic president, visited every station looking for new program ideas.

"NET was thirsting for something different that was not the heavy arts and humanities thing," says Jim Case, the first program manager at KRMA, Denver. He helped create the *Ragtime* series and directed all of its programs. "They wanted something a little lighter. So I invited Marvin Hall, a KRMA producer, and Morath to make a pilot."

Hall, a writer and actor from California, had been stage manager for the Cripple Creek melodramas and was a friend of Morath. Case hired Hall soon after KRMA moved into its new studios in 1957. The twenty-second educational station on the air, KRMA was the first to operate in studios built expressly for TV production. KQED in San Francisco was making programs with two Dumont cameras in a warehouse, and WGBH was operating in a Boston skating rink with a bumpy wooden floor. All three stations made programs for NET distribution. But for a while KRMA had the edge, with new studios and equipment as well as a production crew that Case describes as "incredibly talented."

"It was Hall's idea," says Case. "He knew that Morath understood the history of the period [1890–1920], its popular music, and how to play it. Hall's job was to help Max make the transitions from performer to narrator, from pianist to historian. Our working title was 'Before Jazz.'"

"The educators were using TV as a verbal medium," says Hall. "I thought we should be using visual and dramatic means, performers not teachers, to get the material across. NET needed a person who knew the history of his work, someone who could really connect with an audience. So I said to Max, 'Let's try it. They'll *pay* you!'"

"So," Case continues, "we raided several antique shops, put some ferns on the set and pushed tacks into the piano pads to give it that rinky-tink sound. Max, dressed in his '90s costume, played and sang for fifteen minutes while we rolled the video. I sent the pilot off to New York and back came a contract for twelve half-hour shows."

The series describes a wide range of popular music, most of the hits and a lot of the misses. Along the way, Morath talks about music for silent films, sheet music publication, the emergence of the gramophone, barbershop singing, Tin Pan Alley, and composers like George M. Cohan and Scott Joplin, among many others. He made clear, however, that his first love was ragtime, a musical form that defined the period and influenced most of the popular music that followed.

An awareness of the venturesome nature of the series, its entertainment value, may have encouraged Morath and Hall to pack the programs with information. NET's publicity department also seemed sensitive about this series in which "show" clearly dominates "tell"; its initial press release begins, "A series of twelve unique educational and cultural programs . . . ."

As Morath explains, "NET wanted to get away from the professor in front of the gray drape, but not *too* far away. It's worth a reminder that in those days all NET programs had to have some sort of educational cachet. There was a consultant from the Colorado College music department built into our budget." (No one remembers seeing the consultant.)

In his history of public television, *The Vanishing Vision,* former NET president James Day recalls, "NET needed to reach beyond the converted to find a new audience whose appetite did not necessarily tend toward the acquired tastes of high culture. . . . *Ragtime Era* was everything educational television was not supposed to be: upbeat, fun, and entertaining."

As Jim Case remembers it, the production schedule was exceptionally rigorous, making demands that he enjoyed: "We all came in at 8 A.M. The designer and scenic artist, two brilliant people, had been up all night preparing the set (they sometimes *painted* Oriental rugs on the floor). The station went live at 11:45 A.M., so we had to be out by then. Max had written and memorized the script. There were no cue cards or teleprompters. We walked it through, had a rough camera rehearsal (there was singing and dancing in nearly every show). Then we would just do it, from beginning to end, no stops.

"No one could edit video satisfactorily in those days, so it was like a live performance. The only time we had a bad glitch, we went back and did the entire show over again. We made twelve programs in twelve weeks.

"By the time we were three or four programs into the series we began to get this wonderful reaction from NET. It was what they wanted. It looked like commercial TV."

According to a contemporary account in the *Denver Post,* "Morath sometimes stumbles on words or fluffs lines, but they stay in the show. His fresh delivery gives the appearance of being ad lib."

Looking at the programs today, nearly forty years later, the viewer is struck by two characteristics—the extraordinary amount of information in each program and the intensity Morath brings to his work. In episode No. 2, "Any Rags Today?," we are ushered into a posh "sporting house" by a tall young woman in a feather boa and slinky, sequined dress. Here we find Morath playing an upright piano with its front removed. He is in his customary chalk-striped trousers, a shirt with sleeve garters, string tie, fancy vest with gold watch chain, a derby perched rakishly on his close-cropped hair, and a cigar clamped between his teeth.

"Scott Joplin should be better known today," he begins, launching into "Maple Leaf Rag," the first of six numbers in the half-hour. Between these performances we learn about Joplin and several other rag composers, hear an explanation of syncopation ("ragtime's key ingredient"), listen to some Tom Turpin rags on a piano roll—while Morath puffs reflectively on his stogie—before he shows us to the door as the credits roll. In the episode concerning George M. Cohan, Morath manages to sing and play seven of the composer's songs while throwing in a seemingly off-hand story of Cohan's life and times.

"Morath could go through the camera," says Case. "It was his presence that gave the programs their authority. People believed him. In his narrative he cut right through the center of everything. He used straightforward evocative language that was easy to understand: no bullshit. He was that way in private conversation, too. There were no temperamental problems, no 'motivate me' or 'I don't feel right doing that,' none of that crap. We never had an argument."

In 1959 Case was one of the few people with network experience who was producing for noncommercial TV. He had been an intern at NBC in New York, then worked on several of its major shows—*Howdy Doody, Your Show of Shows,* and others.

"I went to work at the network because I wanted to learn the craft," he says, "and that's where you could do it, in those eight floors of the RCA building. But then I wanted to get out of town. I didn't want to live there or be there because I thought it was not the right environment. I wanted to produce TV programs in a civilized place where there was a concentration of talent. And it all came together in this little series.

"*The Ragtime Era* production was unusual. From 1957 our programs were getting better and better. The chemistry was right. It never lasts long...about four years, then everyone drifts away and it collapses. That happened at KRMA."

For his work as writer/performer, Morath was paid $225 per show. Hall, the producer, made one hundred dollars, and Case earned $125 as director. The studio crew, collectively, was paid $240. NET's total budget for the twelve programs was $22,000. *Ragtime*'s immediate success was reflected in the budget for KRMA's likewise well-received *The Turn of the Century*: fifteen half-hours for $41,000.

Time, Newsweek, and other national publications featured the programs. A Christmas special with Max Morath was produced and offered as a gift from NET to all its stations. Many played it for years. A third series, *The Real West*, was narrated by Morath, who sang and talked about the "true" lives of cowboys. Jack Gould, dean of America's TV reviewers in the early '60s, wrote in *The New York Times* that "[KRMA] could teach Madison Avenue a thing or two...when Morath sat down to illustrate rag piano, his zest and craftsmanship asserted themselves informatively and entertainingly."

In Denver, where initial support for a new educational TV station had been tepid and sometimes hostile in 1956, the *Denver Post* now praised the series' spontaneity, calling Morath, "a ragtime Leonard Bernstein." "He does more than just talk about ragtime on television. He *sells* it," asserted the *Post*, which went on to observe: "In an affluent society, it seems a shame that more money cannot be channeled into educational television."

In 1964, at the high point of his Denver popularity, Max Morath moved to New York and became a one-man ragtime industry, playing club dates, making dozens of recordings for Vanguard and Columbia Records, publishing a collection of one hundred classic rags, appearing on *The Bell Telephone Hour, Kraft Music Hall,* and, for many years, *The*

Arthur Godfrey Show. Having created a successful one-man off-Broadway show, *Max Morath at the Turn of the Century,* he has toured it and its refurbished successors to thousands of communities and colleges throughout the country.

In 1974 Morath reappeared briefly on public television in a PBS special produced by WGBH, *Ragtime.* As the show's host, he is featured along with Eubie Blake (then ninety-one), E. Power Biggs, and Gunther Schuller's youthful New England Conservatory Orchestra.

Here Morath, still slender and energetic, with a few more wrinkles in his smile, is confident and even more facile as he banters with the other performers, introduces songs and dances, and talks about life in 1905 as if he lives there part-time. Blake, with an enormous bow tie and a head resembling a beautiful piece of polished mahogany, plays his first composition, "Charleston Rag," from 1899, his long, slender fingers flying over the keys.

Watching Morath's 1959 and 1974 videos in sequence, it is evident that authority had begun to overtake intensity, In both programs, however, as Case observed, he cut to the center of things.

"I'm not about to retire," says Morath today. "Retire from what? I haven't had a steady job since 1959, and that was in a saloon. I have a mammoth concert tour planned for this season" (1996–97).

He had paused briefly in his career, however: in 1995, he became a full-time student at Columbia University where, in the spring of 1996, he received his master's degree in American studies. The subject of his dissertation was Carrie Jacobs Bond, a publisher and composer in the early 1900s. Bond wrote, according to Morath, two of the most popular songs of all time: "I Love You Truly" and "The End of a Perfect Day."

Soon after producing *The Ragtime Era,* Marvin Hall received a fellowship at the Yale Drama School. He later joined the staff of NET, and then moved to San Francisco where he worked for KPIX and made training films and commercial videos. Hall, who has changed his first name to "Moss," now lives in Pebble Beach, California, and writes travel articles.

In 1964 Jim Case was appointed director of Los Angeles' new station, KCET. Later he became associated with KPBS, San Diego, and produced dozens of documentaries for public TV (including *The Naturalists*, a series that was rerun nearly as often as *Ragtime*), finally returning to Denver to head his own production company. These days, nearing seventy, he plays golf and, as he says, is "writing children's books with more enthusiasm than skill." He credits much of *The Ragtime Era*'s success to video recording and the ability of KRMA to use it skillfully.

But Jack White, now in his eighties, disagrees with the vigor that characterized his presidency of NET thirty-five years ago. "Jim Case was a stickler for quality," he says. "But we bought the series because it was fun, it was clean and fun."

Whatever the elements of its appeal, the series hugely expanded NET's audience. After its initial release NET made a circumspect and prescient, if somewhat awkward, report to the Ford Foundation, the philanthropy on which its future, and that of public broadcasting, greatly depended: "*The Ragtime Era* may ultimately be responsible for greater good to a greater number of average TV viewers than many NET programs of greater intrinsic value."

In 1960 Jack White had good reason to look for programs that enlarged NET's audience. Commercial interests were bearing down upon educational stations and challenging dozens of the FCC's noncommercial channel reservations around the country. Many observers were beginning to question the use of broadcast TV to serve small audiences with educational material. White found what he sought in *The Ragtime Era*, an undeniably entertaining series with enough information to make it an acceptable educational venture. It conclusively tipped the education/entertainment balance, opening the door to *The Great American Dream Machine*, *Masterpiece Theatre*, *Great Performances*, comedies from Britain, Mark Russell's satire and, in 1968, a name change: "public television."

KQED

In his history of public TV, *The Vanishing Vision,* James Day recalls that the first year of KQED/San Francisco, 1953, was nearly its last. Its headquarters was in the back seat of a station wagon. Day, the president, and a staff of eight had managed to keep the station on the air, but the board, alarmed by its increasing debts, had decided to call it quits. Day argued successfully for one more month to raise enough money to reorganize, to bring the Bay Area's corporate leadership onto the scene.

Friends donated a few thousand dollars, a public relations organization was hired, and an all-night telethon was held. Net gain: six thousand dollars, not nearly enough. With the thirty-day grace period about to expire, the PR firm proposed a drastic solution: stage a twenty-four-hour TV auction. The idea seemed crazy. But as Day remarks, "skepticism surrendered to desperation." The now-exhausted staff agreed to give it a shot. After all, KQED had taken its call letters from the Latin phrase "Quod erat demonstrandom" ("that which is to be proven"). A final push toward fiscal solvency seemed necessary.

No one could have guessed that out of the ensuing bedlam of donated barking dogs, chirping birds, and the frenzy of on-air sales, the production crew was creating the mother of public broadcast pledging. The crisis was averted, the KQED Board was reorganized and, more important, as Day says, "We became part of the community." In 1954, KQED got by on $69,500. By 1991, the budget topped $33 million.

Meeting adversity with creative programming was to become a char-

41

acteristic of KQED. The telethon and auction were themselves examples of innovative, attractive live television.

As the *San Francisco Chronicle* reported at the time, "Without realizing it [KQED] put on the best show that has been on a San Francisco station." The telethon had featured, along with civic leaders, physicist Edward Teller and stripper Tempest Storm. During a later auction, someone bought for $250 the (unlaundered) sheets in which Kim Novak had slept the night before at the Cliff Hotel, cut them up, and made them into ties—in which form they were auctioned again. Shirley Temple, a frequent guest, once led the bidding for a boa constrictor. During his auction stint, Dick Gregory remarked, "One hundred years ago I would have been for sale." In 1963, the year WGBH sent its first *French Chef* programs to a national audience via National Educational Television (NET), Julia Childs' cooking knives became KQED's first membership gifts.

KQED was the country's sixth public TV station. When it went on the air it possessed the nation's least promising production facilities, particularly for an organization so determined to create live programs. Its first studio was a dressing room atop the Mark Hopkins Hotel (on top of "The Top of the Mark"), close to its transmitter donated by commercial station KPIX. The quarters were so cramped that in order to frame his subjects the cameraman had to back into an adjoining bathroom.

This site gave way to a trade school where signs in the restrooms above the studio warned, "Don't flush during broadcasts." Eventually, a truck garage was rented (for $500 a month) and converted—with egg-crate acoustic walls—by the staff to a usable facility. Here, however, there were unremovable columns (frequently disguised as trees) in the middle of the studio space.

Throughout this time, KQED produced hundreds of live programs, in some part because its own programs cost less than the ones then for sale (many of its production crew were volunteers). And then there was Jonathan Rice, the program manager, an exceptionally curious, intelligent, and daring producer. It was Rice who urged the creation of live programs seemingly impossible to create in those improvised circumstances—performances of small orchestras and dance and jazz groups, for example. He also offered air time to articulate people—stevedores, artists, mechanics, scientists, politicians, cultists, and cooks.

On the station's twenty-fifth anniversary in 1979, Rice described the projected schedule when the station went on the air: "Of the twenty-three programs, only seven were expected to come from sources other than KQED. Partly because programming available was very . . . limited, educational television consisted largely of high hopes." Those who worked with Rice then speak of his willingness to support their frequently off-beat program concepts and his help in turning their ideas into programs without constant supervision.

In KQED's first live program, Day interviewed Frank Baxter, who had enjoyed great success teaching Shakespeare on TV in Los Angeles. It was the beginning of *Kaleidoscope*, a series of interviews that would run until Day left the station to become president of NET in 1968. *Kaleidoscope* was ideally suited to KQED, to Rice's inquiring mind and Day's informal but persistently probing style. Its early programs featured Buster Keaton, Eleanor Roosevelt, Aldous Huxley, Bing Crosby, Robert Kennedy, Maurice Chevalier, Ella Fitzgerald, and Ogden Nash.

Commenting today on the success of *Kaleidoscope* and similar KQED series, Day gives much credit to San Francisco itself: "It made a great difference. We were in a city that was wide open to new ideas. It attracted talent from around the country. Once we got our name in *Time* and *Newsweek*, people came to us, people who were able to do and say unconventional things." People and their ideas were KQED's chief assets. Very early in its long string of important productions was a debate between Nobel-winning biochemist Linus Pauling and H-Bomb architect Edward Teller. It was seen locally and nationally before becoming one of public TV's first internationally distributed programs.

Rice assigned his secretary, Winfred Murphy, to produce *Kaleidoscope* after Day complained, "I can't keep calling my friends to appear on the show." Several guests were later put to work on their own series. One was Eric Hoffer, the longshoreman/philosopher whose twelve-part

Conversations with Eric Hoffer, produced by Murphy and distributed by NET, created an enthusiastic national audience.

In her unrelenting search for new talent, Murphy learned (from a young studio crew member) about an artist, Takahito Mikami, recently arrived from Japan. She recruited him to demonstrate Japanese brush painting on *Kaleidoscope,* a broadcast that Day says was "distinguished by his inability to understand my questions and my inability to comprehend his responses." Day recalls: "When we finished, Win said, 'Wow, that would make a great series!' I told her she must be out of her mind. I'd been in Japan for two years and I was certain she couldn't find anyone to watch Japanese brush painting. 'I know about that,' she replied, 'but he's cute.'"

In the end, Day suggested she talk to Rice who, typically, encouraged her to try it, with a budget of next to nothing. "I went out and bought hundreds of rolls of pink toilet paper," she says, "to make blossoms for the set. I made blossoms for days."

As it developed, T. Mikami (he apparently thought two Japanese names might be more than an audience could handle, even in San Francisco), proved to be not only cute but an immensely skillful artist and teacher. "He was good," says Murphy, "and he knew he was good. He hated rehearsals, thought them phony, but was flawless in performance."

Japanese Brush Painting became the first of KQED's unqualified hits, both locally and nationally. Its extraordinary success, however, nearly derailed the series before it could muster a full head of steam. The station had put together some brush painting kits—an ink stick, a stone on which to rub it to create ink, a brush, and some rice paper—so that viewers could sketch along with Mikami. The entire staff, including the engineers, sat on the floor putting the kits together. "In no time," says Rice, "I had a corner on all Japanese brush painting equipment in the U.S." The kits were advertised for three dollars. The demand was sudden and overwhelming, requests far outnumbering the kits that could be assembled from existing supplies. Whereupon the ever-resourceful Rice began working the phones until he found a new airline flying to Japan. It agreed to bring in thousands of sets for an on-air credit. (Recently, I discovered the brush painting materials I had purchased from KQED nearly forty years ago, much to the delight of my grandchildren.)

When NET distributed the series it received considerable national attention. In 1958 and '59 an enormous number of people were drawing fish, bamboo leaves, pine trees, roosters, and horses (Mikami also turned out to be a champion rider and polo player). The series sequel, *Once Upon a Japanese Time*, was equally popular. Few seemed to mind that Mikami's drawing paper occasionally slipped off his easel. During one live performance, baby chicks that had been brought in as models escaped, running through the artist's ink and throughout the studio. When it became clear that the brush painting craze had peaked, KQED quickly mounted a new national series on origami, the art of folding paper.

As part of KQED's original staff, Richard Moore was hired as membership director. Moore, who had been a ballet dancer (with Jose Limon) and poet, was one of the early associates of Pacifica Radio and an executive and announcer at its first station, KPFA in Berkeley, where community support for noncommercial radio had been invented. At KQED, he soon became a TV producer and an accomplished filmmaker. As a poet he had been associated with Kenneth Rexroth's anarchist libertarian group. "Coming to KQED in 1952 was my version of going straight," he says.

It was Moore who suggested the series *Eastern Wisdom and Modern Life* and recruited its host, Alan Watts, who had been presenting—also at Moore's request—a regular Sunday morning program on KPFA entitled *Way Beyond the West*. Those who may have considered Japanese brush painting an esoteric and unlikely alternative to commercial TV (until its undisputed popularity) must have been truly bemused by *Eastern Wisdom*, another one-person presentation.

"Alan Watts was very intellectually important to me and others," says Moore, "both at KPFA and KQED. We thought there should be opinions expressed that were not the products of western civilization. I remember bringing him into the KPFA studios and telling him the programs needed to be exactly fifteen minutes long. I asked him if he wanted a countdown. 'Oh, no,' he said and ad-libbed a perfect fourteen-minute, thirty-second program. Quite astonishing."

Watts, a former Anglican priest and leading exponent of Zen Buddhism in the U.S., illustrated his talks with Asian art objects as well as drawings and diagrams that he created with Chinese ink and brushes. By far the most impressive production element in these half-hour programs was Watts himself, with his deep and resonant voice, his piercing eyes and graceful movements. Though many viewers may have understood little of what he said as he examined contrasting concepts in Eastern and Western philosophies, few would forget his enthralling cadences and riveting presence.

Watts was born in England in 1915 and educated at Kings School in Canterbury. He published his first book (of many), *The Spirit of Zen,* when he was twenty, three years before he came to America. His slight British accent and ascetic features did nothing to diminish his attractiveness. By the time he began his talks on KPFA he had been a guest professor at Cambridge, Harvard, and Northwestern universities and dean of the Academy of Asian Studies in San Francisco.

Alan Watts' KQED debut on June 1, 1959, followed *Kaleidoscope,* by now the station's most popular program. "Death" was its singularly inauspicious premier theme. Sitting in the lotus position, Watts discussed the wheel of life and the Buddhist idea of reincarnation. It was, most agreed, mesmerizing. Once again, KQED had created a success from what many thought was improbable material. The audience grew as Watts contrasted Hindu, Buddhist, and Taoist concepts of physical and moral pain, Zen gardens, Zen in fencing and judo, and the relationship of Zen to psychiatric techniques.

For audiences on the cusp of the counter-culture '60s, these were pregnant topics. In some sense Watts brought to Zen what Max Morath was then bringing to ragtime music (*The Ragtime Era,* produced at public TV station KRMA in Denver): a command of his subject, a quick wit, and an intensity that many would (and did) call "showmanship."

Moore and Watts, near neighbors in Mill Valley north of San Francisco, were friends for many years. "As much as I respected him," says

Moore today, "he was not in the same league [intellectually] as Lew Hill [founder of Pacifica]. By the time he got into his second year at KQED, I began to have misgivings about Alan's increasing interest in his self-image and the softening of his inquiring mind."

Alan Watts continued to write and lecture long after his *Eastern Wisdom* series had been run repeatedly on the public TV circuit. The Library of Congress has fifty-seven of his programs in its NET archives collection. His son, Mark, now distributes the videotapes as well as a large number of audio cassettes through his San Francisco company, Electronics University.

Richard Moore would eventually succeed Day as KQED's president and later become president of KTCA in St. Paul–Minneapolis. He produced a wide variety of programs for KQED, nearly all of which were distributed nationally: *Jazz Casual* with Ralph Gleason, which set the standard for such series; Monterey Jazz Festivals; the only TV program ever made with John Coltrane; and film documentaries such as *Take This Hammer* (about racism, with James Baldwin); *Love You Madly,* a profile of Duke Ellington; *Losing Just the Same,* on ghetto life in Oakland; *Louisiana Diary,* about voter registration; and one of the first helicopter fly-over programs, following the California coast from Mt. Shasta to the Mexican border. With funds from the National Endowment for the Arts, Moore once produced a ballet in the open air of San Francisco's Ghirardelli Square. It was choreographed by Merce Cunningham with sounds (the crackle of taxi radios) arranged by John Cage and entitled, not inappropriately, "Assemblage."

Moore made 110 film documentaries at KQED, most of them for NET distribution, after he and Day established the Special Projects Unit across the street from KQED's main studios. He describes its independence as "a great advantage," adding, "Neither Jon nor his staff ever forgave me." Of all the programs, he believes the *Poetry USA* and *Writers in America* series will have the most lasting influence because of their continued use by colleges and universities, and says the Ellington documentaries, including *Sacred Concerts,* were the most interesting because of Ellington himself.

○ ○ ○

Rice reflects upon Moore's penchant for odd subjects: "He hated any-thing that was familiar. He would drive me crazy wanting to do things that often didn't seem to make any sense. He didn't want to do any-thing typical."

"When I got there, Dick Moore was the great creative force," says Candyce Martin, a former CPB staffer who now heads her own produc-tion company, Crossways. Martin was hired by KQED in 1964, when she graduated from Stanford.

"When I arrived, San Francisco, and KQED, were in the throes of the '60s: flower children, rock music, drugs, experimental drama, political protests, encounter groups. We were trying it all.

"But one of the most extraordinary things about KQED was the vol-ume of production. When I was there we were putting out twenty-two programs a week, live or onto tape. Everybody did a lot of work. You might produce two or three shows and direct one or two for someone else. All the producers were jammed into one large room. At opposite ends were private offices for Jim and Jon. For a year, I shared a desk with Tony Smith. He was brilliant." (This was Anthony Smith, then a BBC producer, sent to KQED on a fellowship. He was later one of the architects of Britain's Channel 4 and is now president of Oxford Uni-versity's Magdelan College. Another fellowship employee was poet-writer Maya Angelou.)

By the late '50s, KQED had moved to larger quarters from its original offices, described by one staff member as "three rather tacky offices above Woolworth's." But its production studios, even in the '60s, re-mained inadequate. *Time* Magazine, while describing KQED as "the best noncommercial station in the country" (of 149 then on the air), re-ported that its studio was in "three splintering wooden warehouses near San Francisco's Skid Row."

Local personalities continued to be pressed into service to host dozens of programs, most of them live and back-to-back: the "Hop, Skip and Dance" kids would be ushered out the door just in time to make room for the *Who's Who at the Zoo* animals. Mortimer Adler's *Great*

Ideas would very nearly blend with *Profile: Bay Area,* hosted by Casper Weinberger (later Ronald Reagan's Secretary of Defense). The station sold several hundred thousand copies of the study guides accompanying Laura Webber's *Folklore Guitar.* A national series on semantics was presented by S. I. Hayakawa, and Ansel Adams hosted *Photography, the Incisive Art.* Edward Teller taught a physics course.

In a 1967 feature headlined "KQED Rules Mkt. in Creativity," *Variety* quotes a local commercial TV executive: "I don't know how they do it. I don't know how they can get away with it."

Jonathan Rice, now eighty and completing his most recent term on the KQED board, remembers, "I have this image of Cap Weinberger and Alan Watts—now there's a funny combination! But give them a one-minute cue and they could both end their shows with a perfectly phrased paragraph. There are very few people who can do that. My talent, skill, or good luck was to be able to do things with minimal tools or the wrong tools."

KQED was now hitting its stride, and still improvising. Most of the sets were dressed with furniture from the homes of staff members and furnishings from the Salvation Army. Rice was still making parts for sets in his home woodworking shop. Frank Baxter (who Rice says was his chief inspiration to join noncommercial TV) observed that "KQED is held together by faith, adhesive tape, and capillary attraction."

A visitor to the station in those days entered a sometimes harassed but usually relaxed and always informal environment in which creative and energetic professionals and volunteers seemed to be participating in a nonstop party. In fact, there often were parties. Once, in a demonstration of high spirits, Tom Borden, the art director who routinely turned cheap materials into elegant sets, poured thirty martinis into plastic bags and tied them with red ribbons to a tree outside the studio. "There are so many nice people around here," remarked a staffer at that time, "it's surprising that anything gets done."

In the '60s, several stations in the burgeoning noncommercial system enjoyed greater financial stability and production resources (WGBH in

Boston and KRMA in Denver, to name two), but KQED was both the envy and pride of them all. Its success was due partly, as both Day and Rice explain, to its location. But more important was its highly creative staff and the management styles of Day, Rice, and Moore.

Day, a graduate of University of California at Berkeley, had spent five years in the Army, two years with the NBC-owned radio station in San Francisco, and another two with Radio Free Asia. He had also lived in Japan as part of MacArthur's Army of Occupation, teaching new NHK radio employees how to produce local news and public affairs programs. On the day he resigned from Radio Free Asia (a CIA operation), he was asked to become KQED's first president. "Jim was the sort," says Candyce Martin, "who would come in on the weekends, when the place just got too untidy for him, and start cleaning the Venetian blinds or cleaning out the refrigerator. There was no job Jim wouldn't do, but he never interfered, there was no micro-management."

Rice grew up in St. Louis, a self-described "spoiled brat," the son of rich and creative parents. His mother (who donated a thousand dollars when the station nearly went broke in 1953) loved music and was vice president of the St. Louis Symphony. His father (whom Rice describes as "creative and daring," words Day has used in talking about Rice himself) was a lawyer who loved the wilderness and fishing.

"As a child," says Rice, "I didn't do anything well—not girls, or studies, or sports." At Stanford he enrolled as a pre-law student, but his extracurricular work on *The Stanford Daily* changed his life; he switched to journalism. "I think everything I've done since has been a result of that change. All of my jobs have been the result of being able to write and take pictures."

He became a major in the Marine Corps, a combat correspondent, and, following World War II, a professional journalist, heading the news division at commercial KTLA in Los Angeles. He came from KTLA to become KQED's second employee and remained program manager for twenty-seven years before beginning a long process of partial retirement, finally leaving as a staff member when he was appointed to the board.

Day has described their lengthy partnership at the station as "firmly rooted in our shared interests and a tacit understanding of respective roles: I didn't want his job and he didn't want mine."

"I was totally free," Rice confirms, "to cancel a show or continue it. Jim never interfered. I had total control . . . no committees. I was once sitting at home watching a live discussion between the writers Yevtushenko and Anaïs Nin. They were arguing about who was more honest. It was so interesting I phoned the station and told the director to let it continue another half-hour, to cancel what followed. We were open to ideas from every source and I had a very good idea about what people would watch."

In 1972 Rice won public TV's prestigious Lowell Award. "For the most part," he said then, "our schedule is made up of programs we enjoy and believe in, that we find interesting or illuminating or moving."

Both Day and Rice were experienced and confident, qualities that allowed them to nourish creativity in others, to encourage staff members to, as Day recently reflected, "reach beyond themselves."

A 1968 *TV Guide* story credited the station's "freewheeling attitude" for a large part of its success, and quoted Rice: "The difference between KQED and other stations is that we take far more chances. If you always have to be right, you don't do much."

Looking back, Winfred Murphy says, "A TV station is like a plant; you need to nourish it. Without nourishment, without love, it won't grow or be successful.

"Jim and Jon didn't respond to political influence in the usual ways. The things I've seen turn national executives to jelly didn't seem to affect them. This was great for staff morale. There was no in-fighting and the kind of nastiness I've seen in other broadcast organizations."

One of KQED's last major contributions to both public and commercial TV in its early years grew out of a news format hastily devised during a weekend in 1968, following a local newspaper strike. Known initially as *Newspaper of the Air*, reporters were hired off the picket lines (at one hundred dollars per week), each assigned a major story to relate, and then expected to answer questions.

Mel Wax, a reporter for the *San Francisco Chronicle*, was its host and moderator. Everyone sat in shirtsleeves around a long table. An editorial cartoonist created drawings as the program progressed. It was an immediate success, and KQED was suddenly thrust into the news business. "When [the program] began," recalls Candyce Martin, "most of us dropped everything else and worked on the show. We were down there seventeen, eighteen hours a day. To put out a nightly news show took the entire staff."

When the strike ended after nine weeks, KQED secured a $750,000 Ford Foundation grant—thanks largely to Fred Friendly, a former CBS News producer and a Ford adviser—to keep it on the air in a refurbished format. By this time, local San Francisco restaurants were reporting a sharp drop in customers during the 7 to 8 P.M. broadcast slot. The rechristened *Newsroom* lasted nine years before rising costs eliminated it. In this time it had an impressive influence upon both local and national TV news reporting. The format was soon exported to other public TV stations including KERA, Dallas, where Jim Lehrer moderated the daily programs.

As more public TV programs came on the air, NET and its successor, PBS, had wider choices for their nationally distributed program packages, and more programs were imported from abroad, particularly from England. In 1970, when the number of public stations reached two hundred, KQED was one of seven to be named a "major production center." Its *World Press* series joined *Sesame Street, The Advocates, Mister Rogers' Neighborhood, Washington Week in Review, The Great American Dream Machine*, Wiseman documentaries, and Kenneth Clark's *Civilisation* in the national schedule.

New stations joining the PBS network no longer faced the empty program shelves that confronted KQED in 1954. Indeed, KQED itself no longer felt pressed to create local programs. Plenty of problems remained but the necessity to produce programs was not at the top of the list.

Dick Moore resigned from KQED in 1972 and formed an independent production company with Lawrence Grossman (later president of PBS) before moving on to KTCA in 1981. There he became director of special projects before taking over as president and finally retiring in 1990. He now lives north of San Francisco, continuing to write and publish poetry in, as he says, "national, but obscure, magazines." He gave up long-distance running last year at age seventy-five.

Moore recently reflected upon public TV, program production, and his tenure at KPFA, KQED, and KTCA. "There's a big difference between breadth of vision and running a public television station. KPFA, and to a lesser extent KQED, were simply means of exercising one's interest in many things, the arts and public affairs particularly. That's a very different attitude from most managers who don't think in programming terms, or are not qualified, frankly, not having the educational or intellectual background, to say nothing of the openness of mind or curiosity. Translating broad visions into programming was very much a presence at KPFA and KQED in its early days."

KQED was exceptionally industrious in its first two decades. But it did much more than turn out an astonishing number of programs. In the 1950s and 1960s its productions were defining what educational television was and what public TV would become. As James Day has written, "if what we invented bore very little resemblance to . . . the commercial networks, the difference was entirely deliberate."

5

WETA and the
Battle of the Spanish Armada

When you are very young, good fortune often seems part of the normal course of events. It was the end of a hot summer in 1954. I had been in New York looking unsuccessfully for a job in TV program production. Everyone of any importance was too busy to see me. A friend with a car offered me a lift back home to Cleveland if I didn't mind stopping in Washington for a day where he had some business.

While waiting for him I overheard a conversation about people in D.C. trying to start a public television station. Willard Kiplinger, founder, president, and editor of the *Kiplinger Letters* and *Changing Times*, was mentioned as the leading enthusiast. Someone made a phone call and twenty minutes later I was in his office. He was the first president of anything I had ever met.

He sat at his desk in shirtsleeves behind an ancient Underwood typewriter. Also on the desk was a large fish bowl, half-filled with pennies. Under unruly white hair his puckish face wore an expression of mixed innocence and deviltry. I remember thinking that he looked like a cheerfully successful gambler.

In about seven minutes he had my life's story. He too had been born in a small Ohio town. He and some others were attempting to put a noncommercial TV station on the air. Would I, he asked, be willing to risk six months of my life to produce a series of programs on a commercial channel to demonstrate the benefits of this kind of programming?

I don't think I overstated my qualifications or experience. There really wasn't much of either. Mr. Kiplinger said he would put me on the staff of *Changing Times,* but this would be a "cover." My actual job would be to work with the major constituents of the Greater Washington Educational Television Association (GWETA) to produce, with each one, a program of its choice. When dealing with the Smithsonian, the Library of Congress, the local universities, the Folger Shakespeare Library, and the National Gallery, I would need to follow each organization's lead. GWETA had been incorporated the previous year and could not afford disaffection among its membership.

The pay wasn't much, and there was no production money except what I could persuade each institution to spend on its own half-hour program. WMAL, owned by the *Evening Star* newspaper, had offered air time and a production crew. The programs, nine of them, would be produced live, leaving no room for mistakes.

"Would this interest you?" Kiplinger asked. Now that he had outlined its dimensions and conditions, it must have seemed nearly as daunting to him as to me.

Before I answered, he asked if I would like to donate some pennies to his collection. Fumbling in my pocket for change, I inquired, "What's the charity?"

"No charity," he replied, smiling. "They're my pennies."

I didn't know how to take this, but I was impressed somehow. I said I'd be happy to take the job.

(I later learned that Mr. Kiplinger kept the pennies for children visiting his office. He would invite them to reach in and grasp as many as possible with one hand, and then he would give them a brief lecture on the value of pennies.)

In thirty minutes I had settled much of my future: moving to Washington where I would raise five children and spend the next forty-two years in public broadcasting.

To say that none of us knew what we were getting into does not begin to characterize the next six months. Faithful to the Kiplinger assignment, each organization was invited to choose its own program subject.

With a couple of exceptions (the energetic and creative Father Gilbert Hartke of Catholic University was one), few of the GWETA representatives had the remotest idea of what television was about.

Looking back, we were pretty lucky. The National Gallery wanted a Rembrandt show ("The Life of Holland"). There was, of course, no money to originate a production from the Gallery itself; reproductions were brought to the WMAL studio. Catholic University settled upon a scene from Shakespeare's *Richard III*, featuring Phillip Bosco, who later became an accomplished stage and screen actor. The Library of Congress wisely chose "The Life and Times of Matthew Brady," the Civil War photographer—a tall order, but with the Library's vast photo archive it came off reasonably well. There were other university programs on household finance (American), medicine (Howard), the value of studying foreign languages (Georgetown), and from George Washington University a program entitled "Galaxies in Flight" hosted by eminent physicist George Gamow. William Hines, then editor of the *Sunday Star*, agreed to introduce each program.

The series was scheduled to begin December 13 and run on successive Mondays at 9 P.M., an unusually generous hour for what in those days was called "public service time."

A planning session with the Folger Library kept being delayed—dangerously, it developed, as it began to appear that the Folger's program might need to lead the series. Somehow this failed to trouble me. When I thought of it at all, the gauzy image that came to mind was a visit with a charming and distinguished Shakespearean scholar who looked and spoke like Alistair Cooke with wit and erudition for exactly twenty-eight minutes while gently holding a few of the Bard's priceless original folios.

After sifting through WETA's records I now suspect that the Folger may have sent a list of tentative programs and that I made the final choice. While this is at least possible, what I recall is the following:

I found myself sitting across from Louis B. Wright, then director of the Folger, in his comfortable, book-lined office. When we finally got around to a precise subject for the Library's TV premiere, Dr. Wright turned slightly in his chair and, elbows on its arms, gently pressed the pads of his fingers together, looking away from me through steel-rimmed spectacles. He remained in this contemplative position, silent, until I began to wonder if he had fallen asleep with his eyes open; a dedicated scholar in the act of searching an enormous storehouse of Elizabethan history.

"I think . . ." he said, just audibly, bending forward slightly as if to secure the decision. "I think," he repeated and again hesitated. By this time I, too, was leaning into history.

". . . the Battle of the Spanish Armada," he said, turning once again to me as people do when they reach unshakeable conclusions.

It was the only time in this experience that I betrayed Willard Kiplinger's trust.

"But there's only half an hour," I spluttered. "You want to do the Battle of the Spanish Armada in *half an hour . . . from scratch . . . live?*"

The lapse did not jeopardize GWETA's solidarity, for I am reasonably certain that Dr. Wright neither saw nor heard me. His mind was clearly fixed upon the summer of 1588, on Elizabeth, on Drake, and the ships of Spain maneuvering for attack.

"If the Spanish had won," he said presently, addressing me as the undergraduate I had rather recently been, "the United States would now be another Latin American country."

"Sea Battle" was scheduled to open the series. Dr. Wright volunteered to create the script. And I began to worry seriously. I recall reporting my Folger encounter to my GWETA colleagues, Elizabeth Campbell and Patricia Oliver, both passionate noncommercial TV supporters. (Elizabeth Campbell, founder and vice president of WETA, worked tirelessly for the station then as she does now at age one hundred.) Their response was a tribute to their unfailing encouragement and loyalty to the cause. They beamed. Elizabeth said it would "make a marvelous beginning."

Preoccupied as I was with production details, I became nonetheless increasingly edgy as we approached our first on-air date. More was riding on this enterprise than I had imagined. There were only eight "educational" stations on the air in 1954 (there are now 365 public TV stations), but the local press saw a new one for Washington in FCC-reserved Channel 26 just around the corner. Washingtonians, it was suggested, were thirsting for the cornucopia of programs such a station would bring. "No other city could match the program material available in the nation's capital," said the *Sunday Star*, calling the emergence of noncommercial TV comparable to the invention of the printing press. Our "pilot series" would prove it.

I remember little of Dr. Wright's script. Press reports planted the suggestion that the audience would need to brace itself for Queen Elizabeth's swearing. This advance publicity, touchingly naive by today's standards, was cooked up by a journalist at the *Star*, then owner of WMAL-TV.

Elizabeth Neimeyer, a young woman on the Folger's staff, was recruited to play Elizabeth I in a strawberry-colored wig set off by a large ornamented pearl borrowed from one of her associates. Dr. Wright, a stickler for detail, insisted that we add twenty-six years to Ms. Neimeyer's age through the application of so much make-up that none of us was certain that she would be able to speak, much less swear.

My contribution was a chart of the battle area drawn on a large thin piece of cardboard supported by two carpenter's horses. I purchased several dozen small magnets and glued some tiny, unconvincing ship models to them. Each magnet had a twin on the underside of the cardboard diagram. As Dr. Wright read his stirring account of the Spanish vessels' defeat and the camera concentrated upon the Armada and the English defenders, I was on my back, hidden by the cardboard, moving both magnetized navies.

Rigid with nervousness, sweat streaming into my eyes, it's no wonder that the engagement seemed confusing. For one electrifying moment I became uncertain which naval force was which. Later, and worse, my undercover magnet manipulation momentarily scrambled the ships thoroughly.

In his later report to readers of the Folger's *Journal*, Dr. Wright wrote: "We've had a fling at education by television and whether it educated anybody else, it certainly gave us food for thought.

"We found ourselves enveloped in a 'show' complete with actors...

[the script] was accompanied by a lot of props including a fleeing Spanish galleon on a tricky sea that must've puzzled better seaman than the Spanish commander." He went on to object to the "factitious hokum" and warned—presciently, perhaps—that "[educational TV] is in danger of becoming just another huckster's show without a Madison Avenue budget to slick it up."

Lawrence Laurent, the *Washington Post*'s TV critic, quoted Wright at length, then observed that while the program had to conform to commercial station standards, historical accuracy was not sacrificed and that Wright seemed to be objecting to "television techniques being substituted for techniques of the lecture hall."

Thanks to Elizabeth Campbell and many others, GWETA survived the Armada and much more to go on the air October 2, 1961. WETA's subsequent record of distinguished programs long ago eclipsed its well-intentioned but unpromising beginnings: *Washington Week in Review*, the Watergate hearings, *The Africans*, *The NewsHour with Jim Lehrer*, *National Geographic Specials*, *Talking with David Frost*, *The Civil War*, *Baseball*, and *The West*.

In thirty-five years, WETA-TV has become one on the leading producing stations in the nation's public TV system. Who would have guessed it? Willard Kiplinger, I suspect.

6

The (Improbable) Beginning of Masterpiece Theatre

Near the end of June 1970, Stanford Calderwood and his wife, Norma Jean, were comfortably settled in their regular rooms in London's Claridge's Hotel. Until a few weeks before, he had been executive vice president of the Polaroid Corp. She was an Islamic scholar who took advantage of their frequent visits to England to conduct research at the British Museum.

But this trip was different. Calderwood, bored and affluent but not yet fifty, had left the corporate world, where he achieved success in advertising and marketing, for a life of public service. In the Calderwoods' hometown of Boston, Hartford Gunn had recently resigned as head of WGBH and was moving to Washington to become the first president of PBS. Julia Child, WGBH's famous resident cook and a near-neighbor of the Calderwoods', persuaded Stanford to try for the vacant position. As he set out on this trip, it looked as if WGBH would soon hire him.

Calderwood had considerable experience in acquiring TV programs for Polaroid's sponsorship. He prided himself on buying programs—often documentaries—at what he termed "distress prices" after they had been turned down by other organizations. He also had more than a sketchy knowledge of public television. Polaroid had been an early underwriter of Julia Child's series. "I went into public television, with a long record of squeezing a great deal out of quality programming," he wrote several years ago in a memo provided to at least a couple of researchers.* He had observed the immense success of *The Forsyte Saga*, a BBC adaptation of Galsworthy's novels that had just completed its run on National Educational Television (NET) and thought it strange that neither WGBH nor NET, itself, had any plans to follow-up on its popularity. During his many business trips to the U.K., he had become well acquainted with British theatre and TV drama.

Small wonder then that Calderwood, a restless and aggressive dealmaker, should decide to make a "cold call" on the BBC to ask if they would like to sell programs to WGBH. In the absence of a budget and, as he later acknowledged, without authority from the station, he began to do business. The call from Claridge's set in motion the creation of what would become the most prestigious and enduring drama series in American public television's history. Ironically, the initiative was taken by a man whose tenure in public broadcasting was one of the shortest; Calderwood became the third president of WGBH on June 30, and by the end of November he had resigned.

In researching the history of ideas it is common to discover that many people claim to be the originators of the same concept. Coincidence often plays a large hand in such matters. Frank Gillard was a TV and radio program executive at the BBC, having joined the company as a war correspondent in 1940. He was also, in 1970, a frequent consultant to U.S. public television. In a letter written in 1994 (when he was eighty-six), Gillard describes, in clear and considerable detail, how he gave Stanford Calderwood the idea for *Masterpiece Theatre*. It was during the intermission of a Boston Pops Concert. While the U.S. Congressman seated between them slept off the effects of some warm champagne, Gillard outlined his "Masterpiece" concept. Calderwood, enthusiastic, invited Gillard and WGBH's program manager, Michael Rice, to his house in the country the next day, a Saturday, where they discussed running serialized dramas. Much of Gillard's argument, he

* Other accounts of the early days of *Masterpiece Theatre* citing Calderwood's memo were written by Laurence Jarvik in his doctoral dissertation and in last year's book *PBS: Behind the Screen*.

says, was based upon his concern that no one had planned to build upon the achievement of *The Forsyte Saga.*

"Michael asked me," says Gillard, "to suggest a presenter to give a friendly word of interpretation to the American audience, and I at once nominated Alistair Cooke. . . . So the series was born, and a great American institution was created. I have rejoiced at its huge success."

The concept also occurred to Christopher Sarson, who later became the first executive producer of *Masterpiece Theatre*. In an interview published in the WGBH book commemorating twenty-five years of *Masterpiece Theatre,* Sarson wrote, "I went to Stan Calderwood with the idea [for serial drama]. He just grasped [it]. He reckoned Mobil would be the right company for something like this."

When Calderwood appeared at the BBC he was passed along to Robin Scott, then controller of BBC-2, the chief source of serial dramas. Tall, prematurely gray, and patrician, Scott met Calderwood's brash style and his plan to broadcast large numbers of BBC programs on U.S. public television with skepticism. As Calderwood recalled it, buying programs from the BBC was not easy: "Look, I said, that good stuff sitting in the can is like a hotel room unsold—it's worthless. Why not give us some cut prices and use it as a loss leader?" Scott's answer was to provide a screening room and all the TV drama Calderwood could watch in three days. When Calderwood emerged, there were further talks. Scott, now warming to the prospect of creating a wedge to pry open the American market, thought he might be able to lean on Time-Life, which owned the U.S. rights to BBC material, to sell the programs for less than it would normally expect from commercial TV. Eventually Scott found himself offering a wide range of programming, including the BBC's famous nature and science series. But Calderwood, always the dealer, waved these off with the promise that nature would be next if he got drama going. (An abundance of nature and science programs did flow later, but through a different mechanism.)

In the end, Calderwood left London with several BBC dramas on 16mm film. He recalled later that his enthusiasm was not shared by members of his new staff; WGBH was "a sandbox for overgrown kids," he commented. With the exception of "true believers" David Ives (soon to succeed him as president) and Michael Rice, Calderwood found little encouragement for his interest in importing BBC serial drama.

"I presented my idea of using BBC programs primarily to build an audience for public television," Calderwood wrote twenty-one years later. "The bigger the audience, I argued, the easier it would be to raise money from a broad base of contributors. There were damn few on the staff—at any level—that thought much of the idea."

By this time Calderwood seems to have incorporated in his argument the perplexity that Frank Gillard had expressed: Why not follow-up the success of *The Forsyte Saga*? "In my early talks at WGBH . . . I kept asking that question and failed to get a satisfactory answer. In short, no one seemed to give a damn." In an environment of increasing hostility, Calderwood determined to go it alone.

Perhaps understandably, Peter Roebeck, Time-Life's representative, did not leap at the chance to sell his British inventory at cut-rate prices. Calderwood used the argument that placing a major series on WGBH would be like getting paid to run a commercial for his entire library of programs. "After endless squeezing," Calderwood says, "I finally got what I thought was a price I thought I could raise."

With Time-Life's agreement in hand, Calderwood set out "to cage" PBS. This was comparatively simple. The network was in its infancy, with more hours available than good programs. Sam Holt, then PBS' program head, was delighted by the idea. "This excited me," he says, "because there were a lot of four- to seven-week series. Here was a chance to hook people and keep them. If the audience didn't like a given series, they might miss only a few weeks rather than dropping out of the whole season. We decided to repeat it nationally, giving people a chance not to miss a week."

Calderwood, convinced he had a winner, thought the least of his problems would be finding an underwriter. He was mistaken. Again and again, he reports, he was dispatched from one corporate executive to another, and finally to an advertising agency that would kill the idea.

AT&T was interested briefly, but gave it up. No one would buy in. After some forty attempts he went to the ad agency he had hired at Polaroid—Doyle, Dane & Bernbach. This agency also represented the Mobil Corp. Here he asked Joe Daly to put him in touch with the right man at Mobil. He also extracted a promise from Daly that if Mobil was receptive, DDB was not to kill the deal because no commissions were involved, the chief cause of his failure to raise money elsewhere.

The person to see at Mobil was Herb Schmertz, the intelligent and urbane head of Mobil's public relations and advertising. Schmertz had been a labor lawyer specializing in arbitration before joining Mobil. He was active in the 1960 John F. Kennedy presidential campaign and in the later campaigns of Robert and Edward Kennedy. Calderwood phoned him and asked if he had seen *The Forsyte Saga.* Schmertz, lying, said he had, and that he had loved it. In that case, Calderwood went on, what would he say to buying thirty-nine BBC hours, for about $390,000, to be run nationally. (The final purchase price was $375,000—plus $100,000 toward production costs and $200,000 toward promotion.)

As Schmertz writes in his book, *Goodbye to the Low Profile,* "Even in 1970, that was an absurdly low figure, so I was eager to learn more." Calderwood obliged and soon had a deal, sanctioned by Rawleigh Warner, then Mobil's chairman. Only much later did Schmertz learn that the BBC programs had been shopped around to dozens of other companies.

Mobil's announcement of a million-dollar grant (for both *Sesame Street* and *Masterpiece Theatre*), the largest gift of its kind up to that time, generated considerable publicity.

"This should be clear," says Calderwood, characteristically speaking of himself in the third person, "had Calderwood not met a soul mate in Herb Schmertz, there would be no *Masterpiece Theatre.*"

Schmertz engaged a TV consultant, Frank Marshall, who worked with him on all aspects of WGBH-related projects, including the *Mystery!* serials, in the years to come. These two, together with Michael Rice,

Christopher Sarson, the executive producer Rice had assigned to the series, Sam Holt, and Calderwood himself, met in London on September 21, 1970, to begin screening programs at the BBC. They were joined by public relations consultant Selwyn James, a representative from Doyle, Dane & Bernbach, Peter Roebeck from Time-Life, and the ubiquitous Frank Gillard. Peter Lord and Phillip Jones were their BBC "hosts."

"It was an unusual situation," says Sam Holt. "Both Rice and I had been Rhodes scholars. Sarson, who was British, had been educated at Cambridge. It was a group of Americans far more familiar than usual with British culture, style, and TV than most. We'd been consumers of it."

Sarson was now the most influential member of this expanding team of advisers. London-born, he was thirty-five. He had entered Cambridge to study law and accounting, but after the second year began playing double bass in a local orchestra, became involved as a composer in musicals, and was about to become music director for the Bristol Old Vic when he was offered an apprentice position with the relatively new, independent commercial broadcaster Granada TV. In 1963 he came to the U.S., worked for a year at Washington's WETA, then went to Boston where he was assigned to produce a WGBH series, *Performance.*

The group looked at first episodes from fifteen series, including *Vanity Fair, Portrait of a Lady, Cold Comfort Farm, Middlemarch, Dombey and Son,* and *The Possessed.* Those that survived the first cut were examined further. It was finally decided to lead the series with *The First Churchills.* ("Not one of our best," Frank Gillard remarked years later. "It was beset with internal casting problems.") The decision turned largely upon the lead actress, Susan Hampshire, who had also appeared as the lead in *The Forsyte Saga* and the fact that Americans would be familiar with the Churchill name.

The First Churchills would be followed by *The Spoils of Poynton, The Possessed, Pere Goriot, Vanity Fair, Resurrection,* and *Nana.* As Michael Rice noted in a memorandum to Calderwood soon after the London screenings, "Obviously our backlog for a second season will be much weaker unless the BBC produces some great new shows in the meantime."

Sam Holt later expanded this apprehension: "What we discovered was that we could exhaust the BBC. We spent most of that first week—eight to ten hours a day—screening, and we didn't fully realize that not one in four of the programs would work."

WGBH, Mobil, and PBS had approached the BBC at a time when its management was at the top of its form. Its thirteen-part review of cultural history, *Civilisation* (with $800,000 from the U.S. sources, including $350,00 from CPB), would appear on PBS in the same season as *Masterpiece Theatre*. Again, Sam Holt: "I dealt from the beginning with the four BBC program people. I think they were the most intellectually competent and talented, as well as the best TV management group with which I've ever done business. Huw Weldon was managing director of TV programs and architect of all this; David Attenborough was director of programs; Paul Fox was head of BBC-1; and Robin Scott, controller of BBC-2. Aubrey Singer, because of *Civilisation,* became a kind of special projects guru. Aubrey's entrepreneurial flamboyance had sold the BBC on international coproduction. It had previously been a fairly ponderous process. He proved it could be a cornucopia. BBC coproductions were really cofinancing—'Your money and our production,' as Singer frequently put it.

"David was my nominal peer, but Paul and Robin had the power because they controlled the budgets," recalls Holt. "David Attenborough remains one of the most interesting persons I've ever dealt with: literate, disciplined, distant, extremely smart and well educated, with an enormously fertile imagination and a kind of brutal practicality you hope for in a producer."

While Calderwood was preoccupied by BBC program selection in London, things were not going well for him in Boston. Some of the problems at WGBH threatened to derail the production for which he had now found financing. A segment in a documentary series, *The Ralph Nader Report,* featuring Ralph Nader and his "Nader's raiders" was highly critical of Mobil—"a nasty and damaging scene," according to Calderwood who believed that the producer had gone out of his way to "get at Mobil." He also thought that the producer, Don Fowser, was unhappy about WGBH taking money from Mobil. Calderwood likewise felt that

Fowser's views were supported by the station's staff. Though fuming, Calderwood decided not to cancel the segment, seeing a possible producer press conference on the horizon. Instead, he phoned Schmertz.

"I explained what he was about to get hit with," says Calderwood, "and asked for his understanding. He was very gracious about it. No pressure whatsoever. Again, as the pragmatic man, I wasn't about to put my finger in his eye."

While the Nader program seemed resolvable, another series, *Say, Brother,* WGBH's African-American series, proved fatal to Calderwood's brief public TV career. Initially, the problem concerned language, unacceptable in Calderwood's opinion—the sort that, he said, "chilled the FCC." The difficulty escalated, becoming a racial controversy. The black producer was fired. Calderwood refused to rehire him and, as he says, "My board failed to give me adequate support." (The young producer accidentally drowned before his rehire case was decided.) Stanford Calderwood stepped out of public broadcasting and never returned. "I left," he says, "with no hard feelings."

In the two months before the start of *Masterpiece Theatre*, producer Chris Sarson made several decisions that would mark the series distinctively for years. A musical theme was required, something British and heraldic, music bespeaking the glory of England. What Sarson chose, as it happens, is French. He had heard it years before being played through loudspeakers each morning at a Club Med resort in Palermo, Sicily. Chagrined that a French composition was perfect for the opening, his first reply to inquiries concerning its origins was "Just an old piece I found in the library." A journalist finally identified it publicly as "Fanfare for the King's Supper," by J. J. Mouret, a sixteenth-century, Provence-born musician and sometime conductor of the Academie Royale who had died a pauper. A decade after the TV series commenced, a travel writer assigned to assess the Palermo resort gave it a high rating, remarking that it was even using the *Masterpiece Theatre* theme for reveille.

At the first London screenings, the series' working title was "The Best of the BBC." Soon thereafter, Sarson made some title suggestions to Calderwood. "Masterpiece Theatre" headed the list, followed by "The Best of the BBC" and "This Week's Episode." "I propose just plain 'Episode,'" Sarson explained in his memo. "It has the flexibility and enigma of Somerset Maugham's films *Trio* and *Quartet*.... It's not the catchiest title in the world. I shall brainstorm some more." The final choice was easy; it was the spelling of "theatre" that caused trouble. Sam Holt thought it appropriate but remembers that many public TV station managers seemed miffed that the "re" ending was used. Calderwood, apparently thinking it was Schmertz's idea, says he "choked on spelling it 'Theatre,'" but, again, did not wish to offend the sponsor. For his part, Schmertz says that "Sarson insisted on the British spelling.... I think it was a bit pretentious, but Sarson's view prevailed."

The series required a host, a presenter, someone literate and articulate, to interpret the cultural and literary nuances of a wide range of dramatic adaptations. In England, Ludovic Kennedy, a TV personality and reporter, had expressed an interest. Among Americans, Sarson was working with a list that included Roger Rosenblatt at Harvard, Peter Arnett, a charismatic Englishman at Tufts, William Alfred, also at Harvard, and actor Burgess Meredith. Alistair Cooke was at the top.

Born Alfred Alistair Cooke in 1908 in Manchester, the future *Masterpiece Theatre* host took a Cambridge degree before moving in 1938 to the U.S., where he became a citizen in 1941. He continued his studies at Yale and Harvard and became a foreign correspondent based in America. He worked for a time as a movie critic before beginning the longest-running radio program of all time, his weekly BBC *Letter from America,* eloquent essays on the social, political, and cultural lives of his (now) fellow citizens. For several years Cooke had hosted *Omnibus,* an acclaimed Sunday afternoon cultural TV anthology on CBS.

When Sarson first contacted Cooke, he was writing and presenting a series entitled *America: A Personal History* for NBC. He wanted an Englishman but felt that Cooke was even better "because he was *transatlantic.*"

Sarson's initial phoned overtures failed. Cooke was far too busy. But others, including his daughter, thought it was a splendid idea. Gillard, backing his original idea, phoned Leonard Maill, then BBC's representative in New York, urging him to persuade Cooke to take the job.

With time running out, Sarson visited Cooke on location when he was filming *America* in Boston. The answer was still "no." Still, Cooke could hardly fail to observe Sarson's desperation. Soon after Thanksgiving (which Cooke spent with his daughter, who continued to urge him to host the series), he phoned Sarson. Typically and mischievously he suggested other possibilities—"The person you need," he said, "is somebody with the artful off-handedness of Max Beerbohm, the zest of John Mason Brown, or the talkative guile of Alexander Wolcott." Sarson replied that he agreed but they were all dead. "I know," said Cooke, "I'll do it."

In the next twenty-two years, the courtly, intellectually resourceful Alistair Cooke became *Masterpiece Theatre*, his insouciant and urbane interpretations of the dramas finally becoming an essential dimension of the stories he introduced. After such a long association, Cooke observed, "It was, of course, another element of the magic that I was often blamed for flaws in the composition of, say, *The Mayor of Casterbridge*, *Bleak House*, or any of the scores of masterpieces I have written. It is an impeachment I have learned to live with down the years."

The *Masterpiece Theatre* stage was finally set. But on opening night its most popular programs—*Upstairs, Downstairs, I Claudius, The Jewel in the Crown*—had not yet been produced. Few in the first Sunday audience would have guessed that they were watching the beginning of the longest-running drama series in television's history. At WGBH and PBS the producers worried that it might not survive *The First Churchills*.

The Upstairs, Downstairs Years

On the twentieth anniversary of *Masterpiece Theatre*, Alistair Cooke, its weekly host from the start in 1971, reflected upon its longevity: "After all these years and a succession of about fifty acknowledged hits, a score of near-misses, and one or two nameless flops, the program's steady viewers may be forgiven for assuming that [it] took off like a rocket. . . . Not so. The first effort, if not exactly aborted, fizzled into orbit and limped to earth after twelve anxious weeks. (Somebody—the producer or the writer—was so disheartened that the usual thirteenth episode was never written)."

Christopher Sarson, *Masterpiece Theatre's* first executive producer, concedes that this "first effort"—*The First Churchills*—was not the strongest drama to lead the series. Its selection was based largely upon public familiarity with the Churchill name and the fact that its leading actress, Susan Hampshire, had starred in the much-praised *Forsyte Saga.*

The First Churchills was not based on a literary classic, Sarson says. "It wasn't even a terribly good script, wasn't very well shot, and the action behind the wigs and masks was pretty lousy." Despite such misgivings at WGBH, *The First Churchills* proved to be a popular success, earning Susan Hampshire an Emmy award for best actress of the 1970–71 season.

The calculated risk had paid off. Hampshire was thirty-one when she played Sarah in the programs that followed the lives of Winston Churchill's seventeenth-century ancestors. Scripting problems were compounded for her during the production as she had undiagnosed dyslexia. She would return to *Masterpiece Theatre* several times, winning further awards in *Vanity Fair* (Becky Sharp) and *The Barchester Chronicles* (Signora Madeline Vesey-Noroni).

The First Churchills was followed by ten additional serials in the first season, including *The Six Wives of Henry VIII,* produced by Mark Shivas and Maurice Cowan, and *Elizabeth R,* starring Glenda Jackson.

"We ran them together, six Henrys and six Elizabeths," says Sam Holt, then head of PBS programming. "I still consider this the most brilliant season of *Masterpiece Theatre. The Tudor Cycle* was followed by *The Last of the Mohicans.* Some people thought this programming was bizarre, but it worked. In terms of audience we really did a job. From the fall of '70 to the spring of '72, we roughly octupled our audience."

Holt was involved in another aspect of the new series: its underwriting image. "Now that it's *Mobil Masterpiece Theatre,*" he remarked recently, "it's strange to remember that PBS once decided that companies could not use logos. . . . I would not allow Herb [Schmertz] to use the red 'o' in Mobil against the blue background. Turning Herb down was one of the first hard calls on the PBS underwriting front."

The active participation of Schmertz, Mobil's representative, in creating and sustaining *Masterpiece Theatre* was a solace to some and a considerable concern to many. Some thought his presence during screening sessions when programs were selected represented the sort of corporate influence critics of public broadcasting have always feared. Not only was he outspoken in these program reviews, but he and his TV consultant, Frank Marshall, purchased and commissioned programs that later ran on commercial TV. At least one of the dramas he set in motion, *Disraeli,* ran on *Masterpiece Theatre.*

Holt comments upon the early days of Schmertz's involvement: "I give Herb full credit. He was terrific to work with. Very supportive. I never observed a specific case when he turned anything down on his own. He was not the most obfuscatory individual; you always knew what he liked. But he never bullied us or pushed us around or said, 'It's all my money.'"

The question seems to be whether Schmertz simply spoke candidly or actually called the shots and made the final decisions. I have not been able to find anyone in public broadcasting who asserts that final decisions were made by anyone except the executives of WGBH. Joan Wilson (who took over Sarson's role as executive producer after the third season), said in a 1978 magazine interview, "Corporate sponsors have never dictated decisions at WGBH. Mobil wanted to run *Jenny* and I didn't. It eventually appeared on PBS [presented by WNET], but it wasn't part of *Masterpiece Theatre.*"

Mobil initially found it difficult to set the right image and tone for the new series, particularly through the posters representing each serial. Its ad agency's first effort for *The First Churchills* presented a huge photograph of Rawleigh Warner, its chairman, over which were the words, "Mobil's Chairman is an Angel," causing Schmertz, he says, "to hit the roof." A second effort's headline read, "Mobil Has Deboobed the Tube." "Worse," says Schmertz, "undercutting the intellectual image we had worked so hard to achieve." Finally, Schmertz and his staff took a hand in creating an ad that satisfied them and established an image that would characterize subsequent advertising for each serial, including posters that became collectors' items, covering walls of public television offices throughout the country. It featured a large picture of Hampshire as the Duchess of Marlborough and the headline, "Winston Churchill's Great, Great, Great, Great Grandmother." "That," says Schmertz, "was more like it."

For the others, Schmertz writes in his manual for advertisers, *Goodbye to the Low Profile*, "they violated one of my cardinal principles—you should never attempt to tell the world how great you are. For better or . . . worse, that's a decision people have to make on their own."

Masterpiece Theatre was not without its critics, even as the series rolled through the early seasons, consistently enlarging its audience. Why such dependency upon foreign material? some (including the Screen Actors' Guild) wanted to know. The complaint about imports, especially British dramas, has remained a hardy thorn in public TV's bramble patch from the earliest days.

Schmertz, always the pragmatist, is both annoyed and dismissive: "Our critics would apparently prefer that we practice some form of protectionism or intellectual isolationism. Our support for public television comes out of [Mobil's] discretionary funds, so it is especially important that we get as much for our dollar as we possibly can."

Not the least of the disapproval arose from public broadcasters themselves, who feared that such programming expressed an elite, un-American attitude, or that it would discourage government support of domestic programming. Why can't we create our *own* dramas? others asked. Answers to this are usually lost in the hand-wringing complaints about the cost of mounting drama productions. Lacking in most explanations of why we *can't* is why the British *can*. An important reason why British TV drama is so good and so prolific relates to the U.K.'s theatrical culture, a tradition in which considerably talented actors, writers, directors, and producers move easily among radio, TV, films, and the legitimate stage.

The American fascination with British TV drama, especially that appearing on *Masterpiece Theatre*, has always bemused the Brits themselves, who are consistently exposed to a far greater range of its quality than finds its way to American public TV and cable channels. There is a lot of TV drama in Britain and, until recently, only the thin top slice of it has been exported to the U.S. And that small portion has been seen on *Masterpiece Theatre*. It seemed to occupy a much larger space on public TV schedules because it was, in the main, not only more accomplished than American productions, but was seen in the absence of disruptive commercials, something that can make even modestly endowed TV drama seem compelling.

As a bemused Susan Hampshire remarked about her *Forsyte Saga* experience, "I don't think anyone thought a black-and-white series with a lot of English people in tight bodices and full skirts...would be so compelling to an American audience."

The audience attraction intensified when WGBH acquired, and PBS scheduled, the first of four enormously popular serials, all entitled *Up-*

stairs, Downstairs. They were the first *Masterpiece Theatre* programs purchased from a source other than the BBC—London Weekend Television, one of the two commercial broadcasters that then served London.

In the four years when the fifty-five episodes aired, 1973–74 through 1976–77, there were plenty of other excellent TV dramas on *Masterpiece Theatre,* including the first adaptations of Dorothy Sayers' *The Unpleasantness at the Bellona Club* and *The Nine Tailors.* These were also the years of *Country Matters,* Somerset Maugham's *Cakes and Ale,* and *Madame Bovary,* but all of them were overshadowed by *Upstairs, Downstairs.*

Alistair Cooke tells the story of mentioning to a woman viewer that yes, it was true—Lady Marjorie Bellamy had "really drowned on the Titanic." And he says wryly, "She just broke down."

Upstairs, Downstairs was a phenomenal success both in Britain and the U.S. Today, if you thumb through news clips, reviews, and promotional material, the picture that turns up most often is that of the Bellamy household. It is something out of our TV memory's family album. In the opening sequence of *Masterpiece Theatre,* the camera still glimpses that photo: Here are Lady Marjorie, her dignified husband, Richard, and their son, James. Standing behind them, their loyal servants: Hudson, the butler; Rose, the parlor maid; James, the footman; Mrs. Bridges, the cook; and the others. All stare out at us from their starched Edwardian world, each claiming our attention once again. Much of the charm and success of *Upstairs, Downstairs* arose from the meticulous manner in which the writers followed national events in Britain from 1903 to 1930 and their ingenuity in providing each member of the cast with a distinctive life.

For audiences in Britain and America there was something for everyone. You could identify with the upper-class Bellamys or with the persons "in service" below stairs. The action was sufficiently removed from the 1970s to seem nostalgic but not remote.

Jean Marsh, who (with Eileen Atkins) had developed the story's concept during months of talk over a kitchen table, played Rose. She recalls discussing her choice of this role with her mother—who would have preferred that her daughter had decided to play Lady Marjorie. When Jean pointed out that she knew much more about the working class, having been raised in that environment, her mother objected: "We're not working class!"

"What do you think we are?"

"We're...well...we're *upper* working class."

By the '70s, two world wars had devastated, but not destroyed, the British class system. The Empire had collapsed and service of the sort demonstrated by butlers, wine stewards, footmen, and ladies' maids was to be found only on large estates or in expensive hotels. But when *Upstairs, Downstairs* was playing to its vast audiences, memories of domestic service were still fresh.

The producers dressed the sets with considerable attention to historical detail, and lavished research upon the manner of preparing and serving meals. Paintings on the Bellamys' walls were "authentic." To prepare for the episode in which the King visits the Bellamys' residence at 165 Eaton Place for dinner, consultants from Buckingham Palace were called in for advice. Actors playing both upper and working-class roles took great pains with their accents, costumes, and mannerisms. Thus, when James returns with his stories of the war, when Hazel dies in the flu epidemic, and when Rose loses her young man at the front (and all her savings in the stock market crash), the suspension of audience disbelief is very nearly complete.

Some of this may have been reinforced by backstage crew members, who eventually began to treat the actors playing upper-class roles with greater deference than the others. It was, everyone seems to agree, a lengthy *tour de force* of ensemble acting among persons who were, as Alistair Cooke remarked, "bred, nourished, and polished by the British repertory theater."

Actors in the U.K. are typically as interested in TV drama as in films, probably because of the quality of scriptwriting. John Hawkesworth produced the serials and, with Freddy Shaughnessy, outlined the episodes, working out each thirteen-part serial as a novel, then assigning a writer to each program. Fay Weldon, the novelist, wrote the first one. While it gave them "a big push forward," says Hawkesworth, it was not the right style for further segments.

Hawkesworth, also a successful painter, had been a protege of Vincent Korda, working on films such as *The Third Man* (1949) and *Outcast of the Islands* (1951). He wrote dozens of TV dramas, many of which became part of *Masterpiece Theatre*: *The Duchess of Duke Street, The Flame Trees of Thika, The Tale of Beatrix Potter, By the Sword Divided,* and *Danger, UXB*. It was Hawkesworth's persistence that finally overcame the extreme reluctance of London Weekend TV's new controller of television, Cyril Bennett, to run *Upstairs, Downstairs*. Bennett feared, according to Hawkesworth, that "people will switch off in the thousands," but finally agreed to put it on in a 10:30 slot on Sunday nights.

When *Upstairs, Downstairs* was first screened for the Americans, it ran into a similar problem. Schmertz and Sarson had gone to London to look at a new crop of TV dramas. Sarson balked. He thought it was a soap opera, unworthy of the WGBH series. Also, it was not produced by the BBC which had, up to then, provided all the dramas for the fledgling series. No one could foresee what might result, financially or otherwise, from program purchases that appeared to threaten U.S. public TV's "special arrangement" with the BBC. Schmertz liked *Upstairs, Downstairs* enormously and was never reticent about expressing his opinions. Sarson and Schmertz began a barrage of transatlantic phone calls to WGBH management. Most of these were directed to Michael Rice and David Ives. Ives had become president soon after Stanford Calderwood resigned in late 1970, just weeks before *Masterpiece Theatre* had gone on the air.

Michael Rice was at the center of program decision-making. A former Rhodes scholar and Harvard graduate, Rice had joined the station in 1965, becoming manager of radio and then general program manager. He had been associated with *Masterpiece Theatre* from its inception, suggesting its title and shaping its content. He was a brilliant innovator, fiercely loyal to WGBH.

Schmertz says he told the station that if WGBH didn't want *Upstairs, Downstairs,* he intended to buy it anyway and run it commercially with Mobil sponsorship. "I declared," he writes in *Goodbye to the Low Profile,* "the public will see it for what it is—an intelligent and witty commentary on the class system and a great entertainment."

As it happens, I was in London at this time. As an executive of CPB, I sat in screening sessions and observed the goings-on. We looked at other programming as well as *Upstairs, Downstairs,* including an engaging, swashbuckling serial called *The Onedin Line,* based upon the beginnings of the famous Cunard shipping empire. It featured, once again, the lovely Susan Hampshire and a musical theme by Khachaturian from the ballet "Spartacus." Privately I sided with Sarson although my objections did not match his. I thought *The Onedin Line* was stronger. (In the end, *Onedin* was passed over altogether, later running on public TV through the auspices of the Eastern Educational Network.)

Rice weighed the arguments of Sarson and Schmertz and decided to buy *Upstairs, Downstairs.*

Many years later, after *Upstairs, Downstairs* had proven to be wildly successful, I would sidle up to Chris Sarson at a reception or screening and whisper, "I hear the Brits are selling this attractive Edwardian TV serial that..." And with unfailing honesty Sarson would reply with a smile, "I still think it's trash."

Long after our screening encounter in London, I reminded Herb Schmertz that we had seen *The Onedin Line* together. "Oh, yes," he replied. "That theme always reminds me of 'Stormy Weather.'" He was right, about the theme and about *Upstairs, Downstairs.*

Sarson left *Masterpiece Theatre* soon after *Upstairs, Downstairs* began its four-year run (leaving behind his voice announcement about *Masterpiece Theatre* being "brought to you by a grant from the Mobil Corporation" that remains part of the program in its twenty-seventh season). For a while he devoted his attention full-time to *Zoom,* a major WGBH children's series that he had been developing and finally producing.

"I was exhausted by running two national series," he says, "and too greedy to give either of them up." He finally resigned when a hoped-for raise didn't materialize. "I wanted to get out and flap my wings a bit. I've never regretted it."

Joan Sullivan (later Wilson), a producer on the WGBH staff since 1967, took over *Masterpiece Theatre*. Wilson had been an actress at the Brattle Theatre in Cambridge in the '50s. She came to the station to produce radio drama and then TV programs. From the beginning she made it clear that editing would be part of her acquisition policy and that she was impatient with British programs' slow starts. "We've told the British over and over again," she said in 1978, "that we have a different kind of competition: we really have to capture people's attention in the first three or four minutes." When she decided to cut a scene of two transvestites kissing passionately during an orgy in *I, Claudius* she remarked, "This is something they [the British] get hung up on." During her years with *Masterpiece Theatre* (she died in 1985), WGBH began to assume a larger role in coproduction as well as the acquisition of British drama. Like Sarson, she worked closely with Schmertz at Mobil, recommending final decisions in a constant flurry of forceful memos to the WGBH management. She chose only programs that would have dramatic value to Americans, she said.

Masterpiece Theatre sailed on with new strength gained from *Upstairs, Downstairs*. It achieved the highest ratings of any serial drama since *The Six Wives of Henry VIII,* drawing an audience of 2.5 million in its second season. Eventually *Upstairs, Downstairs* played in forty countries to an estimated audience of nearly a billion viewers.

Jean Marsh's photograph in her frilly parlor maid's cap came to represent the series. She herself toured the U.S. to promote the programs she had invented. She tells the story of a horticulturist asking to use her name for a new rose. She gave permission and a few years later looked for it in a flower catalogue. After a brief description of the "Jean Marsh" rose, it went on to say, "Not good in beds; better up against the wall."

Henry Becton, now president of WGBH, remembers following Marsh in a London receiving line waiting to be introduced to Princess Margaret: "The man attending the Princess presented Marsh as the leading lady in *Upstairs, Downstairs.*

"'Oh,' said the Princess, 'I'm afraid I missed that.'

"The man then described the series in more detail to a still uncomprehending Margaret. 'I'm afraid I was away,' she said, finally.

"'Away!' Marsh replied, 'For *five years?*'"

After sixty-eight episodes (fifty-five aired as part of the series in America), the producer, writers, and cast decided to stop before it began to decline. The London Weekend TV executive who had been so pessimistic about its chances of survival now "exploded," Hawkesworth recalled: "I had an incredible hour with him screaming and shouting and dancing and crawling on his knees, saying, 'Here's a contract for the next ten years! We've got a gold mine that hasn't begun to be excavated yet.'"

At the end, U.S. public TV staged a national fundraiser called "Upstairs, Downstairs Farewell: A Million Dollar Party." Many of the cast were flown to New York then on to Boston to meet large assemblages of adoring reporters and photographers. There were appearances on the *Today* show and a motorcade of Rolls Royce convertibles from Boston's Logan Airport to the Ritz-Carlton Hotel, where a huge press conference was held. The following pledge night featured Jean Marsh and the cast, as well as PBS and WGBH presidents Larry Grossman and David Ives— and, of course, Alistair Cooke. Viewers were encouraged to vote (with their contributions) for "Upstairs" or "Downstairs." (WGBH declared a tie among its local viewers.) The event brought in $1.7 million.

By this time the success of *Masterpiece Theatre* had persuaded public TV producers in New York (WNET) and at WGBH, itself, that some sort of comparable American program production might not be beyond their reach. Sarson says that in the original scheme presented to Mobil he suggested that *Masterpiece Theatre* would whet audience appetites. "We would then," he reflects, "muster our forces and begin a weekly series of our own dramas. The huge disappointment to me was that we didn't turn to American serial dramas."

Sam Holt at PBS also hoped for an American series. He and others felt that American public TV could develop the same sort of drama co-production arrangement with the BBC that *NOVA*, the science series, was initiating at about the same time. Holt attempted to sell Michael Rice on the scheme, encouraging him to talk with Lewis Freedman, public TV's producer of the acclaimed *Andersonville Trial*. Freedman had worked with both BBC and CBC and would have been a good choice. But Rice did not agree. In 1976 WNET produced *The Adams Chronicles,* a thirteen-hour history of Samuel Adams and the Adams presidents, hoping it would rival the British imports. It did not. What's more, its budget of well over $5 million seriously threatened the station's perennially precarious financial position. Three years later WGBH tried its hand with an adaptation of Hawthorne's *Scarlet Letter.* It encountered only modest success. Commercial TV fared better with *Rich Man, Poor Man* and *Shogun,* but CBS failed to create an American version of *Upstairs, Downstairs* with *Beacon Hill.*

When it reached its seventh season (1977–78) *Masterpiece Theatre* had fully hit its stride. *Upstairs, Downstairs* was now part of its past, but *I, Claudius* was in the wings as well as *The Jewel in the Crown* and dozens of others whose substance would grow increasingly contemporary with each new season. By its twentieth anniversary, the series had won twenty-five Emmy awards and consumed nearly five hundred miles of videotape: 121 productions for a total of 740 hours, not including repeats. In 1985 Rebecca Eaton replaced Joan Wilson as executive producer and seven years later veteran *New York Times* columnist Russell Baker stepped into the presenter's role that Alistair Cooke had created twenty-two years earlier. In 1995 the renamed *Mobil Masterpiece Theatre,* the longest running prime-time drama series in television history, was seen on 340 public TV stations by an average audience of just over five million viewers.

Sir Denis Forman, then chairman of Granada Television, was once persuaded to come to New York to promote *The Jewel in the Crown* (with the threat that if he didn't, the public TV audience would think the BBC produced it). While in the U.S. he reflected upon the complications of making the fifteen-hour series: "Always underestimate the public's knowledge of a subject, but never underestimate their intelligence." Clearly WGBH had heeded his advice.

Revisiting Brideshead Revisited

On Monday evening, January 18, 1982, the eleven-part, thirteen-hour television series *Brideshead Revisited* broke over the PBS audience with the suddenness of a storm. Even those who had been enjoying WGBH's *Masterpiece Theatre* for more than a decade were unprepared for this astonishing tour de force, presented by the Boston station's rival, WNET in New York.

In the week *Brideshead* premiered, it was estimated that 60 percent of all the TV households in America watched PBS for an average of three hours. *The New York Times* called it "virtually flawless, avoiding excesses while making every nuance blazingly clear." In the *Washington Post*, Henry Mitchell said, "It is the best series ever seen on American television." *Time*, in a moment of prescience, observed that, "Once hooked, it is doubtful that viewers will give up on the series." Indeed. It caused millions to change their Monday-night habits for the next eleven weeks.

By Valentine's Day, Evelyn Waugh's novel, from which the series had been adapted, leaped to the top of national paperback bestseller lists. Bloomingdale's in New York opened a "Brideshead Revisited Shop" where Bill Blass offered loose-fitting flannel trousers ("Oxford bags") and tie belts for gentlemen and Anne Klein sold low-waisted, pastel linen dresses and long, low-buttoned knit cardigans. On Fifth Avenue, F.A.O. Schwartz did a brisk business selling forty-dollar copies of the teddy bear ("Aloysius") carried by one of the series' leading characters. The *Chicago Sun-Times* and other newspapers published menus of dinners at Oxford in Waugh's time. Plovers' eggs were much sought-after. WNET's publicity files still bulge with over a thousand press clippings—feature stories, fashion notes, descriptions of the lives of everyone associated with the production, architectural reports on the film sites, and . . . more.

Considering the story—a rich, aristocratic British family, obsessed by Catholicism, brought down by self-hatred—it seems surprising that the series should have become one of American public television's greatest hits. (Before its publication, Waugh predicted his novel "would be enjoyed by no more than eight Americans.")

Equally curious was the TV series' financing. For Granada Television, the meticulous production took two-and-a-half years and an estimated $15 million. For WNET, it turned out to be one of American public television's all-time best buys.

Evelyn Arthur St. John Waugh wrote *Brideshead Revisited* between February and June in 1944, while on leave from military service following a parachuting injury. The novel's narrator is Charles Ryder, a man of middle age like Waugh himself when he wrote the book. "My theme," wrote Waugh, "is memory, that winged host." The memories he describes are those of a young man who becomes enthralled, first by an Oxford classmate, Sebastian Flyte, then by Sebastian's sister, Julia, and finally by their irresistibly charming and self-destructive family whose existence is bound to intense religious beliefs and their home, Brideshead Castle. Charles loses Sebastian to alcoholism, later marries, then begins an affair with Julia. His wife leaves him, as does Julia after her father, Lord Marchmain, returns home from self-imposed exile in Venice, to die—but not before confirming his religious faith—at Brideshead Castle.

Timing may have had an important hand in Waugh's recreation of the vivid social environment between the early '20s and the end of World War II. When writing the book in the mid-'40s, he was close to his own experiences and observations, yet sufficiently removed so that they might be transformed by maturity and artistic experience. In the early chapters' description of Charles and Sebastian at Oxford, Waugh's prose is drenched in a roseate glow, a romantic decadence that may have caused him to write later, "Our dreams of the days that are past throw less light on our past than on our present situation."

When he wrote *Brideshead,* Waugh was at the top of his form, having published six previous novels, including *A Handful of Dust* and *Decline and Fall.* He would write fourteen more books before his death in 1966, nine of them novels, but none more memorable than *Brideshead.* It was unique among his fiction as his brother, Alec, himself a prolific author, explains in his book, *My Brother, Evelyn and Other Portraits*: "*Brideshead Revisited* is the only one of his novels in which his poetic side was given a loose rein. He wrote it [soon] after the death of his father, whom he was much like. Is it too fanciful to suggest that death gave him a sense of release?"

Although both Alec and Evelyn dismiss attempts of critics and scholars to match Evelyn's friends with characters in *Brideshead,* there is little question that the extraordinary young men among whom he moved as an Oxford undergraduate—Harold Acton, Cyril Connelly, Robert Byron, and Anthony Powell, to name a few—helped to make the Oxford passages so compelling for readers and viewers.

Like his protagonist, Charles Ryder, Waugh left Oxford six months before graduating. His low grades would no longer sustain his scholarship. Soon thereafter, again like Ryder, he enrolled in art school.

"There was no Sebastian in Evelyn's life," asserts Alec Waugh. Perhaps. But in his last publication, the autobiography *A Little Learning*, Evelyn Waugh describes his romantic attachment to an Oxford classmate he calls "Hamish," remarkably like the fictional Sebastian Flyte: "I could not have fallen under an influence better designed to encourage my natural frivolity, dilettantism, and dissipation . . . Hamish's mother [like Lady Marchmain] made friends with me as a link with her wayward son, and constantly appealed to me to mediate between them; always without effect."

The famous scene in which Lord Marchmain (Laurence Olivier) dies at Brideshead, having at last made the sign of a cross, appears to have been drawn from an actual experience. When John Duggan, stepson of

Lord Curzon, had fallen into a coma, Waugh summoned a priest and saw Duggan, who had been out of the church for years, give signs of faith and contrition. Waugh, believing that his book might one day be adapted, left specific instructions about this scene. The priest, he directed, should be plain, doing his job in a hum-drum fashion.

Despite Waugh's gloomy prediction concerning Americans' reception of his novel, it sold 750,000 copies here, when it was published in 1945. It was welcomed by John Hutchens of *The New York Times* ("Mr. Waugh's finest achievement") but not universally admired. Edmund Wilson, then America's preeminent literary critic, who had previously described Waugh as "the only first-rate comic genius who has appeared in English since Bernard Shaw," was "bitterly disappointed." Diana Trilling told her readers that "when the characters are not wicked, they are silly."

In 1960, William F. Buckley, Jr., who, twenty-two years later, would introduce each episode of *Brideshead* on PBS, asked Waugh to write an occasional column for his *National Review* for a guaranteed five thousand dollars a year. "Higher pay, by far, than we have paid to Max Eastman, John Dos Passos, and Whittaker Chambers," he wrote to Waugh.

"I appreciate that in the circumstances, your offer is a generous one," Waugh responded. "But until you get much richer (which I hope you will soon) or I get much poorer (which I fear might be sooner), I am unable to accept it." The exchange embarrassed Buckley and delighted readers when it was reported by Herb Caen in the *San Francisco Chronicle*.

In October 1946, Waugh went to Hollywood at the invitation of MGM. He had been offered $125,000 for the film rights to *Brideshead*. There was no deal: MGM wanted a love story, Waugh wanted total control over the script. Instead, he spent most of his time writing *The Loved One*, a satire of the California mortuary business, and left for London in February 1947. In 1951, another *Brideshead* project was planned, this time with Graham Greene as screenwriter. But adequate financing was not forthcoming and the scheme fell through.

Just as well, perhaps. "To turn *Brideshead* into a [MGM] two-hour film would be an appalling task," John Mortimer later wrote in *The*

New York Times. "The work would have to be cut so the texture became thin and the 'plot' stood out like a sore thumb. The complex, leisurely flow, which is the great charm of the book, would be lost in a tight 'dramatic' construction. . . . However good or bad, it would not be *Brideshead Revisited.*"

As it happens, it was Mortimer who adapted *Brideshead*, and his script eventually extended to thirteen hours. (He first tried unsuccessfully to "dramatize" the book as if it were a play, without the narrative voice-over that he later gave to Jeremy Irons.)

Granada, one of Britain's leading commercial broadcasters, bought the rights to adapt *Brideshead* and in 1977 assigned Derek Granger as executive producer. Granger, who had been planning to film the novel for ten years, engaged Mortimer to write the adaptation.

Mortimer, probably best known to Americans as the author of the *Rumpole of the Bailey* series and the autobiographical *A Voyage Round My Father*, is one of Britain's most gifted and versatile dramatists as well as a famous defense attorney and prolific essayist.

It had been thirty-seven years since Mortimer read the novel as a student at Oxford. "The book was a part of my life," he says. "I had grown up in much the same way as Waugh. Adapting *Brideshead*, I thought Waugh should have his say. You may find him snobbish . . . or you may bless him as a brilliant and witty writer, who faced difficult problems of faith and duty with commendable courage—but as an adapter you must remain true to him, and that is what I tried to do."

Although the manner in which Waugh himself defined the *Brideshead* story seems relatively simple—"The operation of divine grace upon a group of closely connected characters"—adapting and producing it for television could not have been an easy assignment.

"We hugged the book," Derek Granger later remarked in an interview. "We were true to its faults as well as its virtues." When the most intriguing character, Sebastian, departs for his dissolute life in North Africa, he removes the novel's centrality and focus. Many of the book's most dramatic scenes happen "off stage," and are reported to the narrator, Charles Ryder. Ryder himself is often diffident to the point of vanishing. Jeremy Irons, the actor who plays Ryder, has reported his thoughts when he first read the book: "Is this character going to bore the audience? He certainly bores the pants off me."

While Granada was securing the rights for *Brideshead*, Robert Kotlowitz was dealing with the company as WNET's representative in cofinancing a Dickens adaptation. WNET had supplied the production money for *Hard Times* (most of it from the National Endowment for the Humanities). "They produced, and we learned," Kotlowitz says. "It was a terrific experience for both institutions. I had the okay on scripts and went to Manchester [Granada's headquarters] a lot while *Hard Times* was being made. We decided to produce again as soon as possible."

Kotlowitz, a novelist and former managing editor of *Harper's Magazine*, had first become interested in public television after seeing *The Forsyte Saga*, the adaptation of John Galsworthy novels that was PBS's first great success in 1970. He joined WNET in 1971.

"I was given the *Brideshead* scripts," Kotlowitz recalls. "They were first-rate. However, it's very difficult to tell with a book like *Brideshead* . . . I mean, who could conceive that a story like that would be such a [TV] success? We were told that for an investment of $400,000 we could be coproducers. I knew that Exxon [underwriter of *Great Performances*] moved very slowly; it wasn't going to act soon. I called Jay [Iselin, then president of WNET] from London and told him the price, saying there was no assurance that Exxon would put up that kind of money, that we would have to go out and find it. He said 'Commit,' and I committed."

WNET bought the U.S. rights: four plays in each of three years. As Kotlowitz says, it was "a spectacular example of a risk that really paid off." When WNET signed its contract with Granada, *Brideshead* was planned as a four-episode production. No one could have foreseen how the series would grow or what a huge success it would be.

Derek Granger explains Granada's position: "We wanted to do it without network pressures. PBS was the only possible place for us. We knew that PBS would not question our casting. It was essentially a money-up-front presale, enabling us [to air] the series abroad almost immediately. This is important in creating a great deal of stir."

The north German regional network, NDR, also contributed $300,000 to be "associated" with the production, a deal that soured when, after the series was completed, NDR wanted to cut the number of episodes it would air.

What became the longest production in the history of British film-making began in January 1979 on Malta. In May, before filming was scheduled to commence at Oxford and at the "Brideshead Castle" site near York, labor unions called a strike against all British commercial TV companies, throwing production logistics into disarray. The strike was settled in October but precious summer shooting time had been lost, and all contracts needed to be renegotiated.

Even if production had come off according to schedule, the plans were daunting. They included a full-scale hunting scene, an army encampment at Brideshead Castle, a ship caught in a storm on the Atlantic, and several key scenes to be filmed in Venice.

The first director, Michael Lindsay Hogg, left the production during the strike to direct *Whose Life Is It Anyway?* on Broadway. Charles Sturridge, twenty-eight, an Oxford graduate like many in the production group, was brought in to direct. Sturridge had been a student of Derek Granger in Granada's apprentice program. When one of the actors first met him, he described Sturridge as looking like "an ink-stained little English schoolboy." Later, asked by a reporter how someone so young managed to direct such experienced actors as Laurence Olivier, John Gielgud, and Claire Bloom, Sturridge quickly replied, "Good actors are very easy to direct."

Anthony Andrews, first invited to play Charles Ryder, asked to be considered for the role of Sebastian Flyte because it was such a radical departure from his last TV part, a dashing young officer in *Danger-UXB*, seen on *Masterpiece Theatre*. Andrews' first major role was in the London production of Alan Bennett's *40 Years On* with John Gielgud. He later appeared in several *Masterpiece Theatre* series: *Upstairs, Downstairs; The Duchess of Duke Street;* and *The Pallisers.*

Jeremy Irons had initially been offered the Sebastian part but turned it down for that of Charles Ryder. In the end, both actors were happy. For a time during the *Brideshead* production, Irons was also acting in another film, *The French Lieutenant's Woman*, opposite Meryl Streep. Here he was an older, bearded "Charles." At the end of each day's shooting in Oxford he would dash to the *French Lieutenant's Woman*'s production site in London for night filming, reappearing the next morning in Oxford.

Irons had wanted to become a veterinarian but lacked the grades to enter a school for this profession, so became an actor. After graduating from The Old Vic Theatre School, singing and playing guitar for London theater-goers at Leicester Square, and acting with the Theatre Royale in Bristol, he landed his first major role as John the Baptist in *Godspell*. Like Andrews, he also acted in *Masterpiece Theatre* series— *Love for Lydia* and *The Pallisers*.

The reclusive father of Charles Ryder was played by John Gielgud, who was then celebrating his sixtieth year in British theatre. He had played *Hamlet* five hundred times and had been knighted in 1953. In a review of *Brideshead*, the *London Standard* said Gielgud's performance would "make hard-working young actors writhe with envy." (The same might have been said of his cameo appearance in the 1997 film, *Shine,* sixteen years later, when Gielgud was approaching his mid-nineties.)

When he played the part of Lord Marchmain, Sebastian's father, living in Venice with his mistress, Laurence Olivier was among many friends in the *Brideshead* production. He had not, however, appeared together with Gielgud since a 1935 production of *Romeo and Juliet*. He was well acquainted with John Mortimer, having appeared not long before with Alan Bates in Mortimer's *A Voyage Round My Father.* In 1956 Olivier had invited Claire Bloom (who plays his estranged wife, Lady Marchmain, in *Brideshead*) to act opposite him as Lady Anne in *Richard III*. Her many roles had included those in *The Lady's Not For Burning* with Richard Burton, *Ring Round the Moon* with Paul Scofield, and Chaplin's *Limelight.*

Diana Quick, thirty-four at the time of the *Brideshead* production, spent twenty-one months playing the part of Julia, Sebastian's older sister and Charles Ryder's mistress. She too had graduated from Oxford, where she had been president of its prestigious Dramatic Society.

At the end of the production, Anthony Andrews observed, "If we had to do it over there would be no way we could ever bring a cast and crew like that together and work for two seemingly interminable years...."

Sturridge directed from October 1979 until May 1980, when the production was interrupted again so that Jeremy Irons could complete his assignment in *The French Lieutenant's Woman*. Filming resumed in August and, to everyone's great relief, was completed in January 1981.

One of the series' most memorable cast members is Castle Howard, an eighteenth-century house that stood in for Brideshead Castle. Somewhat ironically, the house was owned and leased to the company by George Howard, chairman of Granada's broadcasting rival, the BBC. Sturridge says that at first the house was meant to seem awesome, then more like a home, and finally a dominating presence.

The castle had been designed by an army captain and amateur architect. Commissioned in 1699, it was first occupied sixteen years later by Lord Howard's ancestor, Charles Howard, the third Earl of Carlisle. Lease income from Granada helped George Howard restore many of the castle's rooms (he reckoned there were between 130 and 140) destroyed by fire in 1940. Christopher Sykes, Waugh's biographer, acknowledging that there were several contenders for the model for Brideshead Castle, says that Castle Howard with its five-mile private drive, its fountain in front, its tower, dome, and tall entry was the one Waugh probably had in mind. Some parts of the castle are open to the public and there is a small restaurant, but the private quarters still house the family. Waugh was a frequent visitor at grand country estates, and a snob, as many have observed, occasionally lowering his two-foot ear trumpet out of disrespect for those he considered bores or otherwise unworthy. A journalist visiting the castle after *Brideshead* became popular reported that "Castle Howard was crowded with middle-class summer visitors. If [Waugh] were not dead the thought would have killed him." More to his liking would have been the memory of a woman visitor in 1807 who wrote, "It is better to be a pheasant at Castle Howard than most things elsewhere."

When the series opened in Britain in 1981 virtually all professional critics remarked upon *Brideshead's* sheer beauty: "radiant images of beautiful people, beautiful places, beautiful things, a museum of luminous daydreams." Robert Kotlowitz, remembering his first impression, says "It was gorgeous." Much of the credit for such visual splendor belongs to the production's director of photography, Ray Goode, who, along with Jane Robinson, a leading British designer and theatrical costumer, created sumptuous fantasies based upon authenticity. (The interior scenes on the ship were filmed in the art deco lobby of Mayfair's Park Lane Hotel.) "You can't just design old frocks," declared Jane Robinson. "You have to think about the sort of women they are."

Soon after the strike in 1979 Kotlowitz in his WNET office began receiving phoned reports from Manchester about the enlarged plans for the production—the consequence, he was informed, of "the writers now having time to think more expansively." First he was told that it looked like five hours, then six. Six months later, it had grown to eight, and that was not the end.

"I said," Kotlowitz remembers, "I had no objection to [a greater length], but you have to know that we can't invest any more money. Well, ultimately it was up to thirteen hours and we stayed at $400,000. By then Granada *itself* didn't know how much they had invested. To this day they can't tell you how much the series cost. Once it was made (by then Exxon had committed the original $400,000), Granada came back and said 'Can you help us?'

"Well, it's very hard for public television to say we'll put more money in. Where are you going to put it in *from*? So we managed to get some [more] money together from Exxon—they were very helpful in this situation. It was about $100,000, another 20 percent, not at all significant in terms of the total budget. Granada's investment must have been $15 million ultimately. And there we were for a half million."

Following its U.K. premiere in the fall of 1981, Anthony Burgess, perhaps Britain's most respected novelist, wrote, "I think it is the best piece of fictional TV ever made. It is the book. In some ways, it is better than the book."

The *Sunday Times* called the series "compulsive viewing" and the *Financial Times* told its readers that *Brideshead* was the nearest thing to perfect in the entire history of television series.

This effusiveness was repeated by U.S. critics, when the series opened six months later on PBS. As in Britain, *Brideshead's* appearance precipitated a rash of '20s costume parties and a flood of new scholarly assessments of Waugh's literary works. Newspaper and magazine journalists stood on each other's shoulders to reach for words of praise—"irresistibly seductive," "sumptuously beautiful"—during the series' first run and when it was repeated beginning July 11, 1983.

A handful of writers staunchly bucked the tide of this acclamatory outpouring, their contrarian missives leveled not so much at *Brideshead* as at public broadcasting and the Brits. To wit, this widely reprinted excerpt from Jonathan Yardley's column in the *Washington Post*: "Once again we gullible Yankees have been taken in by the crafty Limeys. We've been duped! It's just a British bore, a soap opera for the educated and moderately affluent gentry that gets its politics from public radio and its economics from Louis Rukeyser. Give us a smidgen of Eton and a dollop of Harrod's, toss in a thigh of Princess Di, and we writhe in our near uncontrollable ecstasy."

One generally acknowledged negative aspect of WNET's production was the addition of remarks by William F. Buckley, Jr., following each episode. They were frequently dismissed or put down as mistakes. In a column titled, "Sloppy Shirt-tales on a Neat Show," *Newsday* critic Marvin Kitman compared Buckley to the character Bridey, Sebastian's older brother: "He has a certain lack of humor about his condition. His face is set in perpetual grimace, a pained expression which is contagious. He even *sounds* more British than Bridey."

With *Brideshead's* overwhelming success in Britain came Granada's full comprehension of what this achievement had cost. The series had been an unqualified hit in England and was almost certain to be an outstanding success in America. Granada again pressed the Americans to pick up a larger share of the huge costs.

It has been more than fifteen years since Robert Kotlowitz faced Granada's appeals and hostility, but even now this extremely reticent man lowers his voice when discussing the encounter.

"Beyond the fact that we had a contract, we were not newcomers to each other," he says. "It was very unpleasant. I came home from that trip [to Manchester] so angry I couldn't even talk about it." Clearly, his meetings with the Granada executives left a deep impression.

In a 1982 radio interview, Jac Venza remarked, "It's going to be hard to look at a ninety-minute feature film again that encompasses a novel of this sweep."

Indeed, it seems unlikely that another series like *Brideshead* will come our way soon. Its secret of success is no secret: take a first-rank novel, have it adapted by an experienced writer whose unique literary skill and sensibility matches his understanding of the theater's dramatic requirements, assemble a cast of immensely gifted performers supervised by a seasoned producer who is able to communicate his intense dedication to the author's story and a director who inspires confidence, employ the best technicians, don't worry greatly about production cost overruns, and . . . *voila, Brideshead Revisited.*

The language of the drama is somewhat ornate, as it is in the novel, something that Waugh, himself, later acknowledged. Is it "too literary," as some think? John Mortimer says he hopes it is: "So is Shakespeare, Chekhov, and Wilde. American television audiences, accustomed to the doctrine that two minutes is too long a pause between each visual shock, may, perhaps, find this a change and something of a relief."

Mister Rogers in His Neighborhood

"**P**lease think of the children first. If you ever have anything to do with their entertainment, their food, their toys, their custody, their child care, their health care, their education—listen to the children, learn about them. Think of the children first."

That's Fred Rogers talking, the creator of *Mister Rogers' Neighborhood*. He turned seventy in 1998, on March 20. His TV series for children—the longest-running series on PBS—celebrated its thirtieth birthday on February 19, 1998.

It is entirely possible that Fred Rogers is not a saint, but I have found little evidence to suggest otherwise. You needn't take my word for this: talk to the people who have helped him to produce the program since its beginning, ask the children, and adults—more than eight million of them—who view the programs regularly. Or thumb through a 1996 book of essays entitled *Mister Rogers' Neighborhood,* edited by Mark Collins and Mary Kimmel. Here are some of the words you'll find there—written by responsible people in media, social sciences, and the arts—to describe Rogers: welcoming, gentle, dependable, caring, smart, gifted, disciplined, honest, sincere, creative. In the book's foreword, Bob Garfield, columnist and NPR commentator, out-and-out calls him a saint, saying further, "He's an endocrinological wonder drug, restoring metabolic balance to our entire culture."

In the same book, a distinguished educator, Paula Wehmiller, who once went to Pittsburgh to interview Rogers at his production company, Family Communications, Inc., describes her encounter when he walked into the room: "In spite of the bustle of busy office noises on the other side of the door, there is a stillness in this moment, a sense that we have paused in the present tense. I am safe here to be myself. . . ."

That's what I call "welcoming."

While adults are given to a certain enthusiastic gushiness when talking about Fred Rogers, he himself is subdued, a condition he seems to inspire among his young viewers—three-to-five-year-olds, mostly, with a two-to-eight spillover. A lot of grown-ups watch, too, and not just parents of the children's audience. His message, "You are special, and loved" is not lost upon aging people, who sometimes find their self-esteem slipping away. My wife, a psychotherapist, sometimes assigns *Mister Rogers' Neighborhood* viewing to older patients with good results.

Rogers was a quiet, frail, carefully disciplined only child (until his parents adopted a daughter when he was eleven), who spent much of his time alone, playing with puppets, some of which continue to inhabit his programs' "land of make-believe." Respiratory difficulties once persuaded his parents to confine him to an air-conditioned room, in the company of another boy with similar problems, for an entire summer.

Perhaps because of his solitary early life, Rogers remains, despite his TV celebrity, an extremely private, quiet person, a man for whom solitude seems nourishing.

"Solitude," he says, "is different from loneliness. It doesn't have to be a lonely kind of thing."

He is fond of quoting an Italian phrase, *"Chi anda piano, anda sano, anda longtano."* ("The person who goes quietly goes with health and goes far.") Quiet has always been a defining characteristic of his programs, a pleasure for most children and a tonic for their parents. The style is an almost unbelievable departure from most loudly exuberant, frequently violent and fast-cut contemporary programs designed for the same audience. (In cities where the *Neighborhood* follows *Sesame Street,* children might be supposed to experience culture shock from the sudden change of pace.)

"I wasn't allowed to go out of my house by myself when I was little," Rogers says. "My parents were afraid that someone would take me away, and they wouldn't see me again."

He found his most direct emotional expression through music, "Music was my first language. I was at times scared to use words. I didn't want to be a bad boy. I didn't want to show people that I was angry, or rather tell them. But I could literally laugh or cry or be very angry through the ends of my fingers. For an only child I think that was very safe. So this [piano] was my friend."

In a comment that may apply to his own life, he observes, "It may be easier for us if, as children, we were allowed to have our angry feelings and someone we loved let us know that those feelings were a normal part of loving and being loved.

"I must be an emotional archeologist," he writes, "looking for the roots of things, particularly the roots of behavior and why I feel certain ways about things."

The center of Fred Rogers' childhood was a large, comfortable home at the top of Weldon Street in the small, industrial town of Latrobe in southwestern Pennsylvania, a place his biographers unfailingly describe as the home of Arnold Palmer and Rolling Rock beer. Rogers, himself, in the style of one of his puppets, Lady Elaine Fairchilde, calls it "one of the garden spots of the world." Here his father, James, owned and operated a prosperous brick factory, one of several enterprises initiated by Fred's grandfather, Fred Brooks McFeeley. His mother, Nancy, had a strong interest in music and drama.

For many years, until he began to object seriously, he was removed from school between January and April to accompany his mother and grandparents on their annual visits to Florida, leaving his father to tough it out in Latrobe. "The biggest issue was leaving my father," he says now, remembering their long-distance phone calls.

He speaks of his parents with respect but somewhat distantly, the way someone might remember a dignified aunt and uncle. Clearly his greatest affection is reserved for his grandfather. It was Fred McFeeley (known as "Ding-Dong" in the family) who argued that young Fred should be encouraged to run along the tops of walls, who brought him "neat things" to inspect, and helped him order things boys like from the Sears catalogue. Each summer he spent a few precious days on his grandfather's farm where he was allowed to ride an old horse and told that he was loved simply because he was himself, someone special.

In his 1994 book *You Are Special*, Rogers writes, "My grandfather was one of those people who loved to live and loved to teach. Every time I was with him he showed me something about the world or something about myself that I hadn't even thought of yet."

Fred McFeeley Rogers. (How many sensitive men have McFeeley for a second name?) The McFeeley name also lives on, of course, as a character in the *Neighborhood*, the "speedy delivery service" postman.

Rogers spent a year at Dartmouth before transferring to Rollins College in Florida, where he majored in music composition and graduated in 1951. Much to his parents' dismay, he gave up plans (temporarily) to enter a Pittsburgh seminary and, saying he hated what he saw on TV, went to New York, where he was hired by NBC. In the next two years he became an assistant director for *The Voice of Firestone* and a floor director for *The Lucky Strike Hit Parade,* the *Kate Smith Hour,* and a cowboy program for children that starred Gabby Hayes. It seems odd to think of Rogers working on these high-powered network shows. He never refers to his own productions as "shows," always "programs." Still, he seems to have learned a lot from this brief encounter with commercial TV. He frequently repeats Gabby Hayes' response when asked how he managed to think of millions of children watching him: "I never think of millions," said Hayes. "I concentrate on just one little buckaroo."

In 1953, the year after his marriage to Joanne Byrd, a pianist and fellow graduate of Rollins, he returned to Pittsburgh to help organize WQED, the nation's first community-supported public TV station. Here he developed a daily, one-hour program called *The Children's Corner,* which initiated many elements of today's *Mister Rogers' Neighborhood. The Children's Corner,* hosted by a young, impish Pittsburgh actress, Josie Carey, lived for seven years, giving birth to Daniel Striped

Tiger and King Friday XIII, puppets that Rogers brought to the studio from home. Rogers produced the program, worked the puppets, composed the music, and (with Carey) wrote lyrics, but never appeared on camera. Although they would agree upon "themes," Carey's lengthy and free-wheeling conversations with the Rogers-manipulated puppets were entirely improvised.

"Are we having an intellectual conversation?" Carey asks Daniel Striped Tiger in one episode, when the dialogue began to falter.

"I don't know, are we?" responds Rogers, the voice of Daniel.

"Yes," says Carey, now beginning to giggle nervously, finally laughing uncontrollably (this was *live* TV), her little flat hat slipping off her head. To watch those programs today is to revisit the innocence of children as well as the charm and artless naivete of '50s television.

In the ephemeral world of TV programming, most of it controlled by skittish ad agencies and jaded producers on their way up or down the job ladder, the sustainability of any series is always in question. Professional loyalties are rare. Uncharacteristically, many of the people associated with *The Children's Corner* productions remain with Fred Rogers more than forty years later. The sneakers into which he changes on the program are themselves hold-overs from the earliest days, when he dashed quietly back and forth behind the scenery to work the puppets.

During the *Children's Corner* years, Rogers began studying child development at the Arsenal Family and Children's Center, established by Benjamin Spock and Erik Erikson. There he met Margaret McFarland, a child psychiatrist, perhaps his most important mentor, with whom he consulted almost daily until her death in 1987. "Somehow," says Rogers, "early on, I got the idea inside of me that childhood was valuable, that children were worthy of being seen and heard, and who they were would have a lot to do with how our world would become. Childhood goes to the very heart of who we all become."

He also commenced night and weekend classes at the Pittsburgh Theological Seminary. In 1962 he was ordained by the Pittsburgh Presbytery with a charge to continue his work with children and families through the media.

In 1963, with program awards—including one for the best local children's program in America—coming in, Rogers was invited to Toronto by the Canadian Broadcasting Corp. (CBC), a considerably more sophisticated production facility than Pittsburgh's "educational station." Here he created a children's program called *Misterogers* under the supervision of Fred Rainsberry, the inventive and durable head of CBC's children's programs. "I've seen your rapport with children here in the studio," Rainsberry told him. "Now I want you to talk with them on camera."

The series incorporated a "Land of Make-Believe," a toy trolley to take audiences there, and Rogers' newly composed song, "It's a Beautiful Day in the Neighborhood." Rogers himself now appeared at the beginning and end of each program. It became a hit throughout Canada. But after a year Rogers left the network to return again to WQED, where his fifteen-minute *Misterogers* became the half-hour *Mister Rogers' Neighborhood*—essentially the same program we see today. In 1964, it secured financial support from the Sears Roebuck Foundation, making the program available to all public TV stations. In his eighth decade, with more than eight hundred programs from the current series behind him, Rogers continues to script several weeks of new programs each year, composing the music and lyrics and, of course, appearing on camera as well as behind the scenes with the puppets.

PBS's first schedule in 1968, one year after Congress passed the Public Broadcasting Act, carried *Mister Rogers' Neighborhood*. In these early years, as now, public television faced a fragile financial future. In May 1969, John Pastore, an experienced and crusty senator from Rhode Island, held hearings on continued U.S. funding. Rogers was scheduled to testify after a two-day parade of witnesses had left Pastore seemingly bored. At stake was $20 million—not much by television standards but enough to give the new enterprise time to organize and attract a national audience.

It was nearing lunch time and Pastore urged Rogers to submit his views in writing. Instead, Rogers talked for precisely his allotted ten minutes about his own program, his hopes for the new noncommercial network, and what it would mean for children. He recited the lyrics from one of his songs in which he encourages children to discover feelings about themselves that can be mentioned and managed, "producing good feelings of control."

At the end, Pastore, obviously moved, said, "I'm supposed to be a tough guy, but this is the first time I've had goose bumps in two days. I think it's wonderful. Looks like you've just earned the $20 million." And the hearing room filled with applause.

Over the years, the *Neighborhood* has become so familiar that we may fail to appreciate its logic and the effectiveness of its detailed construction. Roger Townley, a teacher and writer, has compared the program's form to the theme and variations of a musical composition, A B A C A:

(A) Rogers enters his room and settles in.

(B) He leads us on an excursion to a bakery or craftsman or zoo, where things and ideas are gathered for the dream ("make-believe") sequence.

(A) These are brought back, inspected, and discussed. We are introduced to the "dream" and go into it.

(C) In the "dream" itself, puppets play a central role.

(A) We return to reflect upon it.

Every element has meaning and is there for a purpose. The most obvious, perhaps, is Rogers' arrival, singing his opening song, changing into his informal sweater and sneakers. "Now," he seems to be saying, "I'm all yours. This time is for you"—in most children's lives, rare behavior for an adult. Lately, I've noticed a new instance of "business": just before he hangs up his sport jacket, he holds it up in front of his face and immediately lowers it. Peek-a-boo, of course. He smiles and goes on. But he's also taking a split-second opportunity to demonstrate disappearance and reappearance, leaving and returning— reassurance so important in a child's life. We do not remain in "make-believe," we always return to reality. ("Reality," says Rogers, "is the stuff that dreams are made of.")

The programs' unvarying form, their fairy-tale-like style and substance, make them easy targets for caricature, and Rogers himself an opportunity for parody, as Johnny Carson, *Saturday Night Live,* and many comedians have discovered. "I always saw real affection in those spoofs," says Tom Shales, TV critic for the *Washington Post.* "In a way it's an honor.... It shows he has become an institution in America, not just on TV. It's a cultural event, not just a show."

"The matter of transitions," Rogers says, "is one of the most important aspects of the whole thing." This means preparing children for change, allowing them space to comprehend and make connections. In a world increasingly dominated by a surfeit of data served up instantly through electronic communication, adequate time to make some of life's most important connections has been greatly diminished. A teddy bear (or King Friday XIII) may be an important transitional figure in a child's life. The trolley that takes us to "make-believe" and back is one of the *Neighborhood's* most significant transitional vehicles. Rogers' change into informal clothes, stopping to feed his fish when he moves from one room to another, the camera tracking him through the model neighborhood after he leaves for an excursion—these devices help children to make logical connections.

On a recent program, Rogers tells us that Mr. McFeeley will soon deliver his dog to be looked after for the night. So we follow him outside onto his porch where he sits on a wide swing and waits, thinking about the dog's visit. Typically, it is very quiet. He calls our attention to this (after a silence that seems interminable, even on *this* program). He comments upon the swing's squeak. Mrs. McFeeley comes by with a parrot in a cage. We look closely at the bird and there is more discussion of the dog's visit. Mrs. McFeeley leaves and her husband finally arrives with his dog.

Some years ago at the prestigious international Prix Jeunesse children's TV program competition in Munich I sat bemused after a screening of a *Mister Rogers' Neighborhood* episode as one European TV producer after another registered astonished disbelief that such a slow-paced, quiet program could find a place in U.S. television—or *any* television. The

American program they viewed with approval had been produced by a children's cable network and featured a spectacular food fight.

Those who have watched Fred Rogers' programs for nearly three decades have seen some changes: there are more excursions now, the family of puppets has been enlarged, and, although still maintaining their determinedly simple exteriors, their personalities have changed slightly just as real people evolve. (Rogers remains the voice of King Friday, Daniel Tiger, Queen Sarah, Henrietta Pussycat, and the feisty Lady Elaine Fairchilde.) And there are "theme weeks" during which a variety of life's traumas and vexations become the program's substance: loss, learning, divorce, competition, sharing, and growing all are played out in both "make-believe" and reality.

Rogers has also produced a set of eight programs designed for adults—*Mister Rogers Talks with Parents*—on many of the same themes. When Robert Kennedy was assassinated and most TV services were repeating the brutal images of his killing, Rogers worked through a day and night to produce a low-key special program to allay children's fears and comfort their parents.

Many professional observers regard Rogers' music and lyrics as the programs' most attractive and effective elements. The first piano piece he learned as a child was "Play Gypsy" to accompany his grandfather McFeeley, who played it on the violin.

Much of the *Neighborhood*'s music was improvised in an immensely sophisticated manner by Johnny Costa, a versatile pianist who was with Rogers since the beginning of the series. Yo Yo Ma, the celebrated cellist and a frequent visitor to the program, called the Costa-Rogers collaboration "wonderful." Rogers describes Costa as "so gifted . . . one of the most talented jazz pianists in the world, an exceedingly sensitive man." When Costa died in 1996, Rogers seriously considered ending the series. Each program continues to feature Costa's opening and closing.

In his private life, Fred Rogers is a disciplined person: up at 5 A.M. for swimming at a nearby gym, a spare breakfast (he's a strict vegetarian), then a couple hours in his writing room where he reads, writes, and composes on a piano before business at Family Communications, Inc. He rarely accepts social invitations, doesn't go out at night, doesn't watch television, and is in bed by 9:30. His wife is now a concert pianist. "She keeps her schedule, he keeps his," says a friend. "She is a good match for him." They have two married sons and two grandsons.

While not shy, Rogers is hardly gregarious. Some who come to interview him report that they soon find they are talking about themselves, while Rogers snaps their picture with his camera, later sending a note with the photos enclosed. Jeanne Marie Laskas, a columnist for the *Washington Post Magazine,* had this experience:

"He is not what you'd call an eager man when it comes to press coverage," she writes. "You think you're learning about him, but all of a sudden you're learning about yourself. I wanted to write about a man, a human being, warts and all, and instead I kept writing about a saint . . . ."

"It's no secret," admits Rogers, "that I like to get to know people—and not just the outside stuff of their lives. I like to understand the meaning of who people are and what they are saying to me."

In addition to encouraging children to feel good about themselves and teaching them skills such as patience, sharing, and the ability to pay attention, Rogers clearly wishes to convey dependability. In a child's unsure and sometimes frightening world he is there, day after day, reassuringly. "I'll be back," he says at the end of each program, "when the day is new, and I'll have more ideas for you." And he is back. He's been back for thirty years. It is possible that the series' longevity is as important as its substance.

"In the vast sea of television," says Mark Shelton, a neurosurgeon and author, "*Mister Rogers' Neighborhood* is taken as a sort of fixed point, a North Star. Rogers is likeable and trusted because he tells the truth about the outside world, about even the adults who surround children."

"My hunch is," Rogers has written, "that anyone who sustains good work has had at least one person—and often many—who have believed in him or her. We just don't get to be competent human beings without a lot of investments from others."

Tom Shales attributes Rogers' effectiveness and success to conveying that "he really is what he is. His philosophy comes through his actions and words. This isn't . . . what someone hired him to do. . . . At the center of it all is this trust that young viewers place in him . . . the sense that he is not just fooling."

I once read some remarks Rogers made as a dutiful, but reluctant, speaker at a fundraising luncheon for President Bush at Duquesne University in Pittsburgh. I believe there is some connection between the story he told on that occasion and his work all these years for children and public television. Flanked uncomfortably between the President and Senator Arlen Specter, this is what he said:

> I know of a little girl who was drawing with a crayon in school. The teacher asked her about her drawing and the little girl said, "Oh, I am making a picture of God." The teacher said, "But no one knows what God looks like." The little girl smiled and answered, "They will now."

So saying, Fred Rogers disappeared and went back to his work.

10

How They Got to Sesame Street

Sesame Street, arguably the most successful children's TV series ever created, has remained one of public television's most durable leaders for three decades. About ten million people in the U.S.—children, parents, teachers, and care-givers—watch the show each week. Unlike many programs that require months, sometimes years, to find a loyal audience, *Sesame Street* was extremely popular from its first day on the air.

Every three or four years the series is refreshed, its curriculum modified to keep educational and social messages current as it prepares children for grade school. Over the years it has won more than one hundred major awards, including seventy-one Emmys (more than any other series in history) as well as two George Foster Peabody awards.

The accomplishment of the series' producer, Children's Television Workshop (CTW), has frequently received national recognition. In 1998, Joan Ganz Cooney, *Sesame Street*'s creator, received the Presidential Medal of Freedom, the nation's highest civilian honor. However, it sometimes goes unnoticed that the series is seen regularly by more than 100 million children in 140 countries throughout the world. For all of the much-vaunted international attractiveness of U.S. films, TV, and video ($11.5 billion in world-wide sales in 1996), it seems entirely possible that *Sesame Street,* in its quiet way, may be moving toward exerting America's greatest cultural influence abroad. It has now begun to educate children in places such as China, Russia, the Middle East, and Africa. The long-term effect of this may turn out to be much more meaningful than the feature films, clothing styles, and fast foods of American origin.

The concept of teaching basic skills to very young children in the manner developed by CTW was first discussed at a dinner party in New York City. It was February 1966. Joan Cooney and her husband, Tim, were entertaining Lloyd Morrisett, vice president of the Carnegie Corporation of New York, and his wife, Mary. Also present was Anne Bement, a producer at Channel 13, the educational TV station in New York. The fourth guest was Lewis Freedman, Joan Cooney's boss and program manager at Channel 13. Freedman, whom Cooney later described as having "an extraordinary ability to inspire producers on his staff," was frequently present at critical times throughout the early history of public television. A Harvard graduate, he was a highly intelligent and resourceful producer who created some of the most innovative programs for both public and commercial television in the '50s, '60s, and '70s. In 1980 he became director of the program fund of the Corporation for Public Broadcasting (CPB). At his death in 1992 he was director of the William Benton Broadcasting Project at the University of Chicago.

"Lewis was holding forth," says Cooney, "on the educational potential of television. He would dramatize and mesmerize. I was always in his thrall."

On this particular evening Morrisett was likewise especially attentive to Freedman's persuasiveness. For he was aware (and the others were not) that the Carnegie Corporation had recently agreed to support several research projects concerning preschool cognition. Both he and Alan Pifer, then president of the Carnegie philanthropy, each had two small children, and both were extremely interested in cognitive development among preschoolers. During the conversation Cooney described *A Chance at the Beginning,* a documentary she had recently produced for Channel 13. It concerned a federally supported education project for youngsters. It was a modest but successful half-hour program and the U.S. Office of Education had purchased 125 video copies of it for distribution throughout the country.

A few days later Morrisett invited Freedman and Cooney to a luncheon where they discussed undertaking an investigation of preschool learning among disadvantaged children, a study leading to a Channel 13 program that would be broadcast nationally on the stations affiliated with National Educational Television (NET). Clearly Freedman did not want to lose Cooney as a public affairs producer and told Morrisett, "Well, Joan wouldn't be interested," to which Cooney replied, "Oh, yes, I would!"

Remembering the situation years later, Cooney says, "I didn't know I was going to say that until I said it. But I suddenly saw that rather than producing one documentary after another that no one watched, television itself could affect the lives of the poor." But Freedman suggested another person and the opportunity seemed to have passed.

In the next week, Tim Cooney, speaking with Morrisett on an altogether different topic, interrupted the conversation to say, "I know something you don't know: Joan would *really* like to do that project." This appealed to Morrisett who finally paid Channel 13 to release her to conduct the three-month feasibility study. "I never told Lewis," says Cooney, "because I always felt it was a little disloyal. I can't remember if Tim asked me if he could do it. But Tim and I knew that this was absolutely the right thing for me." (Later she said that she would rather have investigated teaching literacy to adults or teenagers. "Preschoolers were not my thing," she says.)

She remembers that she and Morrisett agreed on one thing from the start: thinking of the outcome as a daily hour of television for preschool children.

In June 1966 Cooney began her work, traveling around the country observing children's TV programs. "I hadn't even seen a children's television show," she says, "and the more I saw the less I wanted to see because it was mostly mindless cartoons except for *Captain Kangaroo* which was an okay show but we didn't want to replicate it.

"I had no credentials for this except a B.A. in Education [from the University of Arizona] and having done one half-hour television program on the subject. It was an immense leap of faith for Lloyd to say, 'She's got the brain power to do it. I'm interested in her opinion.' He just decided he was going to bet on me which in a funny way was the single most significant personnel decision that was made."

Cooney's report, with the dissertation-like title "The Potential Uses of Television in Preschool Education," was completed in October 1966 and sent to Carnegie, which in turn distributed it to the U.S. Office of Education and some major philanthropies. The Ford Foundation, which had poured money into educational TV, was not interested. Children's programming was not seen as an important feature of non-commercial television.

In her report Cooney recommended that her station, Channel 13 (WNDT at that time), produce the programs. Jack Keirmeier, then president of Channel 13, met with Cooney and Freedman to discuss it. Twenty-five years later Cooney described the meeting in an interview with Robert Davidson, who had been appointed assistant director of CTW when it was established: "[Jack] looked up and said to me, 'Who are you? I see this "I" throughout the study. Why would anyone be interested in your opinion? I don't mean to put you down but you're not an expert in any of this, and the whole report is filled with "I think," "I believe," "I suggest."'

"It was not a crazy thing to say. I said, 'Jack, I couldn't agree with you more. But there is something called the Carnegie Corporation of New York that is very interested in what I think. I know you think that is very difficult to believe, but it's the truth.' He said, in effect, 'Well I just think that's crazy.' And neither he nor Lewis made any move to get [the production support]. Jack did not see the potential for Channel 13 at all."

Alan Pifer's response to Keirmeier was that it might be for the best since with the budget eventually required the tail would probably wag the dog. By then the initial planning budget of one to two million had grown to four to six million. Channel 13's annual budget was about one million.

The result of the station's disinterest was that Pifer invited Cooney to leave Channel 13 and take a position at Carnegie where she would divide her time between constructing a plan for a TV series based upon her report and helping to form a Carnegie Citizen's Committee on Public Television that eventually made possible the creation of the Corporation for Public Broadcasting, PBS, and National Public Radio.

A lot of ideas of how to proceed with a series were advanced. One, offered by the U.S. Office of Education, suggested making a grant to each of three commercial animation studios, giving each of them a set of educational goals. Each studio would make a pilot program and the "winner" would produce the entire series. In the end, Carnegie arranged a seminar where TV producers could explain their procedures to educators. Here the ubiquitous and persuasive Lewis Freedman stopped the show by proclaiming, "You cannot possibly do this without setting up a [new] organization. There is nothing in the United States that can do this, so you have to create that animal." "We knew it could not be done by commercial TV," says Cooney, "and that we had to take a chance on public television."

In 1967 an important question among potential contributors to what would become CTW was who would direct it. The Ford Foundation felt that a woman would not command sufficient respect. At Ford and other institutions executives were seeking an Important Name, someone like Harold ("Doc") Howe, the respected U.S. Commissioner of Education. Morrisett asked Cooney to prepare a list of potential candidates. He also questioned her about becoming the deputy director on the assumption that she would eventually take over. Her answer was "No." She explains: "I said I was not going to become number two. He said, 'You don't mean that!' And I said, 'Yes I do.' I never would have said that without Tim telling me to say it. In truth, the project was in my head and Lloyd was nervous that I might leave. I said, 'Lloyd, I was born to do this job.' All that confidence." In March 1968 Joan Cooney was appointed executive director of Children's Television Workshop and became president of the organization when it was made a corporation two years later. In 1990 she resigned as president but remained as a member of the board and chairman of its executive committee.

In the fall of 1967 Cooney worked out a merger arrangement with NET and its president, Jack White, in which she and her organization would remain "semi-autonomous." NET would charge no fees for administering CTW (an almost unheard-of agreement in public TV). She would report directly to NET's board. "The deal," she says, "made no sense to me then or now, but Jack White wanted the project at NET." (When she first went before the NET board, she reports, one of its most enthusiastic and supportive members was Peter ["Pete"] Peterson, president of Bell and Howell. He later became U.S. Secretary of Commerce and, in 1980, Cooney's husband.)

In January 1968 Carnegie committed $1 million to the project. The Ford Foundation, more cautious, pledged $250,000, and the U.S. Office of Education $4 million. In March a press conference was held to announce the new organization and its director. Gerald Lesser, a Harvard professor, long-time friend of Lloyd Morrisett and a man with considerable experience in children's TV, was named chairman of CTW's advisory board.

By 1968 the Corporation for Public Broadcasting had been organized by its chairman, Frank Pace, and his associate, Ward Chamberlin. Pace, a former congressman, Secretary of the Army, and President of General Dynamics, had been appointed to CPB by Lyndon Johnson. Cooney visited Pace in Washington, where she was becoming a familiar figure seeking funds for CTW's first year of production. Her description of their first encounter would seem familiar to those who knew Pace, whose avuncular conversational style blended homespun anecdotes with observations reflecting sophistication, intelligence, and an exquisite political sensibility.

"He talked for forty-five minutes without stopping. He said, 'Prove you can do something before you try to do everything. Choose your goals. Don't have any more than four. Prove you can do something.'" The advice, Cooney remembers, was extremely valuable. "We ended up with objectives that were most important. [Meeting Pace] had a profound effect upon what we did that first season." It is of no small additional consequence that Cooney left CPB on that occasion with its commitment to supply CTW with $1.5 million, the projected shortfall in the first year's production budget.

Research was soon in full swing, key staff positions were being filled, and production formats tested. "Luck," says Cooney, "plays an immense role in television. But research proposed reducing luck to a minimum. Mindless cartoons were testing high. Purposive material had to test high. That was the challenge. I kept saying [to the staff] we're going to do a *Laugh-In* [a highly-rated, funny and fast-moving program of that period] for kids. We can't get the inner city kids if we don't reflect what's going on out there. I kept saying 'hip' and 'fast' and 'funny.' I don't know how right I was in retrospect. But I believed it absolutely. And lots of animation, lots of puppets."

Several of the production personnel knew Jim Henson and admired his work. In a staff meeting one of them had remarked, "If you can't get him, don't use puppets." She then remembered that a couple of years earlier a friend, Edith Zornow, who eventually joined CTW, invited her to a small New York theatre to see some TV commercials made by Henson. They were designed for local markets, but not in New York, and featured puppets in ads for products such as Chinese food. In one, a Chinese dragon went through supermarket aisles knocking things over and breathing fire. She thought they were hilarious, roll-on-the-floor funny. And then she forgot about them until Henson's name came up again. "I knew exactly who they were talking about," she says. "I was thrilled." The staff told her they had talked with him and he was interested; there was no need for her to meet him. Soon thereafter, at a seminar at the Waldorf Hotel in New York, she watched as "this bearded, prophetic figure in sandals walks in and sits way at the back, ramrod straight, staring straight ahead with no expression on his face." She turned to an assistant and whispered, "How do we know that man back there is not going to kill us?" He replied, "Not likely. That's Jim Henson."

She refers to her association with Henson as "not an uncomplicated relationship over twenty-five years. It was not a straight love-love relationship but [in the early days] the complications were in the future. *Sesame Street* created all the complications with those guys."

Chief among her new staff was executive producer Dave Connell who had produced *Captain Kangaroo*. He was not easily persuaded to join

CTW in 1968. When he read a description of the new series—heavily informed by research and headed by a woman he had never heard of—he had said to himself, "There goes $8 million down the drain."

"Dave was terrifically collegial," wrote Cooney after his death from cancer in 1995, "a wonderful leader with a great sense of humor, an immensely gifted animation producer who created most of *Sesame Street's* animation in its first season." Connell also produced *The Electric Company*, CTW's second successful series. He eventually became CTW's vice president for production as well as senior producer and writer for its math series, *Square One*.

Testing formats in the early stages of preparing *Sesame Street* was sometimes a trying experience. On one occasion involving a personal favorite of Connell's entitled "The Man from Alphabet," Cooney read her notes to the staff after the screening. "It was inside and cute," she says, "but it didn't work at all." Connell said nothing. "I don't think he was expecting me to give notes to the producers," Cooney continues, "without going through him. I did notice that he didn't speak to me for the next three days."

Several of the original production team have laid claim to the invention of the Big Bird character. Robert Davidson, then CTW's assistant director, says the story of record is that they all sat around while the two-ton canary joke made the rounds. The idea of a *street* seems to have come from Jon Stone (who has also claimed that he and Henson often discussed a bird muppet). "1-2-3 Avenue B" was a suggested title but was thought to be "too New York, too hip, too inner city." Finally there was some panic about finding a title before show time. "We had hundreds on a list," says Cooney. "'Sesame Street' was the least bad, but we didn't like it."

As planning for the series neared completion, attention turned to airtime. Dave Connell and others felt that a morning slot was essential. Jack Keirmeier at Channel 13 was unwilling to part with *any* time. But finally—and Cooney says, "grudgingly"—he proposed 11:30 A.M. Cooney thereupon offered the series to New York's commercial Channel

Eleven, which was quick to accept it at an earlier hour. Selling other public station managers on morning time was no easy matter. Eventually about 60 percent of them agreed. *Sesame Street's* broadcast on Channel Eleven in New York provided a huge metropolitan audience, far larger than had it been aired on noncommercial 13. In this and in some early employment-related matters (one highly recommended and sought-after publicist told CTW he could never work for a woman) Cooney reflects, "The people who said 'no' were very big breaks as well as the people who said 'yes.'"

In September 1969 regular studio production of *Sesame Street* commenced. And on November 10, nearly three years after its concept had first been discussed, the series premiered nationally. It was an enormous success. Cooney and her producers knew that the programs were testing well but no one was prepared for such an overwhelming triumph. At a reception following the first broadcast, Frank Pace was moved to announce, "This is the most important thing since the discovery of the atomic bomb!"

Such huge and sudden public acclaim generated both satisfaction and unforeseen difficulties. "The hardest thing for me," says Cooney, looking back on those first frenetic days and months, "was what happened internally. There was a kind of collective nervous breakdown. Everyone had hung together as a team and had put their egos aside. They were dealing with an idea bigger than themselves. But suddenly everyone wanted credit and wanted their names in the paper." This seems to have afflicted most of the top producers. But even the advisors complained that they were not being interviewed. To one disgruntled staff member who came to her months after the royalties on his work had begun, she said, "Some of us got rich, some famous. Nobody got both."

After launching its first venture CTW's horizons swiftly widened and much of the preoccupation with who was taking credit for what was dispelled by a greatly expanded agenda that included its second popular series, *The Electric Company*. There was much good fortune in CTW's future as well as work that was altogether unanticipated in its early planning days. Robert Davidson remembers receiving a phone call the day after *Sesame Street's* first broadcast. The president of CTV, Canada's national commercial channel, said he wanted to come to New York immediately to purchase the series. "It was astonishing," Davidson says. "None of us had given any thought at all to the utility of *Sesame Street* beyond its domestic use." Three decades and well over one hundred million international viewers later, CTW continues to expand its opportunities abroad—selling the series without changes, providing a version dubbed in the host country's language, and creating coproduced versions in cooperation with foreign educators and producers.

In her remembrance of Dave Connell, written for *Current Newspaper*, Joan Cooney describes the beginnings of *Sesame Street* and the remarkable people who developed it: "The early days were really a case of all for one and one for all. Every member made irreplaceable contributions to our joint experiment. Collectively we were a genius."

11

Fred Wiseman:
No Simple Solutions

As I write these words, Frederick Wiseman's thirtieth film, *Public Housing,* is about to be broadcast, December 1, 1998, through PBS, the national network that has presented all of his documentaries. It concerns the Ida B. Wells housing development on Chicago's South Side. The sites of his past documentaries have varied from high schools to hospitals, from public parks to private playgrounds. He has shown us the inside of military and police units, welfare and model agencies, prisons, a primate research lab, a meat-packing plant, and a zoo.

It is often said that Wiseman's films are about institutions. This is almost accurate. His films are, in fact, about people interacting within institutional settings. People add complexity to institutions that are often poorly and simplistically designed for the purposes they serve.

The style of these films is deceptively simple; most are shot in black and white with one camera and no narration or music. Wiseman, who selects the subjects, is producer, director, editor, and sound technician on location. Later, he distributes the product through his small company, Zipporah Films, in Cambridge, Massachusetts. His television contracts have never permitted editing. This kind of control, together with the energy required to find financing for each film from philanthropic sources, is almost unheard of in contemporary filmmaking. It has made Wiseman what one writer has called "a genre unto himself."

Unlike most people in his profession, he seems to be creating a coher-

ent body of work, an *oeuvre*, as contrasted with a large number of mis-
cellaneous films. He says he did not set out to do this. "But after I'd made
seven or eight films, I realized that I had made one long film and I was
continuing to add segments to it. [They] are all about various aspects of
contemporary American life. It seemed a worthwhile thing to continue."

To characterize him as unique would understate both his tempera-
ment and creative accomplishments. A *Boston Globe* interviewer once
observed, "An easy manner conceals a graceful intellect. It is perhaps
one facet of his genius that he does not appear to be one."

Although he refuses to discuss the intent of his films or to compare
his work with other producers' work (and is resolutely silent on his personal life), he talks about his filmmaking techniques with a candor re-
freshingly removed from movie-making jargon. "People make such a big
deal about documentaries," he told a reporter a few years ago. "A documentary is just another form of fiction. It is arbitrary...made up. It
doesn't follow the natural order. Its major sequences are shorter than
they are in real time. They acquire meaning they wouldn't have in iso-
lation. What's magical about a good film is magical about a good play or
a good novel. If you try to define it, you're a fool."

Tom Shales, one of America's leading film and TV critics, has called
Wiseman "one of the greatest nonfiction filmmakers who ever lived" and
frequently rails against public television (though it has aired his films)
for largely ignoring his importance. "You'd think Wiseman, on the basis
of his record," wrote Shales in the *Washington Post* in June 1986, "should
have carte blanche. But the Reagan-dominated public television bureaucracy would deny composing paper to Beethoven and canvasses to
Picasso." In another column he compared public television's treatment
of Wiseman with turning down D.W. Griffith and Thomas Edison.
(Wiseman, himself, once observed that "the life of public television is
not programming, it's bureaucracy.")

Shales has not been alone in praising Wiseman and condemning
public TV (especially CPB) for its inadequate support of his work. In
1986 Wiseman had the temerity (some said the foolishness) to testify
before the Senate subcommittee on communications, detailing his crit-

icism of public TV and CPB, its largest single source of production money. "Personal politics, the buddy system, jealousy, and pop ideology dominate the [CPB] panel discussions," which he went on to describe as "guaranteeing mediocrity."

At the time, Robert Coles, a psychiatrist, Harvard professor, and accomplished writer, applauded Wiseman in *The New Republic,* both for his films and for "taking on the very people whose power can stand between him and his work and thousands of viewers."

Frederick Wiseman was born in Boston on New Year's Day of 1930. His father was a lawyer and his mother was associated with child development clinics. He graduated from high school in Boston and from Williams College, where he was an enthusiastic student of literature (finding special pleasure in a Williams' course on Stevens, Eliot, Yeats, and Pound), finally taking a law degree from Yale in 1954. In the mid-'50s, he spent a couple of years in Paris enrolled at the Sorbonne.

"I think I went to law school because I didn't know what else to do," he says. "I hadn't thought very carefully about my professional career."

What he had thought about, a lot, was movies: seeing them and making them. For a while he taught law ("Psychiatry and Law," among other courses) for Boston University and was invited by a high school classmate to join a company that serviced government contracts for agencies such as the U.S. Department of Housing and Urban Development and the anti-poverty program. "I was switching to a film career," he says, "but had to earn a living."

In 1964 he produced his first movie. "I had read Warren Miller's novel, *The Cool World,*" he recently remarked, "at a point when I was very dissatisfied with teaching law. I didn't think I could direct it myself because I hadn't had the experience, but I acquired the rights. I admired the movie that Shirley Clark had made of [Jack Gilbert's] *The Connection* and approached her to direct, and that's how it started."

While teaching at Boston University, Wiseman occasionally took groups of law students to observe what was to become the subject of his next film, and first documentary, Bridgewater Prison for the Criminally

Insane, run by the Massachusetts Department of Correction. *Titicut Follies*, shot in twenty-nine days over a period of three months and completed in 1967, is a harrowing look inside Bridgewater where, at the time, many of its mentally ill patients, civilly committed, had no criminal records.

Elliot Richardson, then the state's attorney general, ruled that the film invaded the privacy of the prisoners and prohibited its distribution within the Commonwealth of Massachusetts, a restriction that was in force for twenty-two years until a state court overruled it in 1991. Ironically, Bridgewater's superintendent thought the film might be extremely useful in drawing attention to conditions in the hospital and hasten long-sought funds to correct them.

It took Wiseman six years to pay off the *Titicut Follies* production costs. The litigation it initiated was both lengthy and costly. Still, the film, apart from its acknowledged social importance, established a documentary style that would mark Wiseman's movies for the next thirty years and cause his work to become a distinguished contribution to public television, an enterprise not crowded with first-class filmmakers.

Wiseman's next film, *High School* (1968), documented a large public high school in Philadelphia, and its middle-class teachers, administrators, students, and parents. Here he encountered a problem that would return in some of his subsequent work. When the movie was finished, he screened it for those who had given him permission to make it. They approved of it highly—until the reviews came in. Most of the critics praised Wiseman and made extremely negative observations about life in the school. In *The New Republic*, Joseph Featherstone wrote, "Northeast High School is preaching an ugly and pinched doctrine." *Newsweek*'s Richard Schickle said the school was "moronic," calling the staff "petty sadists" and "simple-minded." A lawsuit was threatened and Wiseman, already appealing the *Titicut Follies* judgment, withdrew *High School* from distribution in Philadelphia.

The problem would arise again in his eighth film, *Primate* (1974), in which he followed the daily activities inside the Yerkes Regional Primate Research Center in Atlanta. After seeing the film, the director of Yerkes, Dr. Geoffrey Bourne, expressed mild concern that a couple of scenes might be misunderstood. Then came public reaction, after which Bourne canceled his appearance on a WNET follow-up program to discuss it, calling the film "rubbish" and "a perversion." (In New York the film got 150 calls, largely negative, and a bomb scare, a threat on Wiseman's life, and a Nielsen rating of 4.7.)

WGBH, Boston, delayed its broadcast of *Primate,* then scheduled a discussion that featured Wiseman, a Yerkes' representative, a Harvard philosophy professor, and Graham Chedd, then producer of *NOVA.* This generated three hundred calls, all bitterly opposed to one or another of the panelists. Yerkes sent out a form letter asserting it had been duped by "camera tricks." At the time, Wiseman defended himself against Bourne's charges by suggesting he was "reacting less to the film than to the reviews."

In a lengthy and informative description of *Primate* and its troubled broadcasting history, David Denby wrote of Wiseman in Boston's *The Real Paper:* "With the savvy of his law background and the tenaciousness of a man repressed by state censorship (the *Titicut Follies* ruling), he takes the time, trouble, and money to get in where it counts.... Reality will speak for itself, but someone must be quick enough to go there and report back."

Given the intimate nature of Wiseman documentaries, it is surprising that he has needed to fend off so few complaints about privacy.

"It's funny," he once told a reporter, "how willing people are to be filmed. For some reason, it never seems to bother anybody. I ask permission if there's time. It's rare that somebody says no. It's a combination of flattery, indifference, and vanity, I guess."

Yet it seems remarkable that in documentaries such as *Hospital* (1969), and especially *Near Death* (1989), where issues of life and death are being decided by doctors and families, people seem to be so little distracted by the camera and sound equipment. In *Near Death,* which Harry Waters of *Newsweek* described as "the most powerful dose of reality ever administered by the tube," it is astonishing that those involved in some of the most poignant scenes are not more self-conscious.

"Most of us," says Wiseman, "are not good enough actors to change our behavior for the camera. If we were, the level of acting on television would be a lot better."

Why did the families allow Wiseman to observe these painfully personal moments? He says they told him they wanted to help him (and, one assumes, the film's viewers) to get through the same ordeals. "So in a sense," Waters wrote, "*Near Death* could be regarded as a rehearsal." In addition to his unobtrusive manner, another reason for his acceptance among the subjects of his films is that he presents himself as a quietly mature and intelligent person. Pauline Kael, long-time film critic of *The New Yorker,* commented on this indirectly in an early review of his work: "There's a good deal to be said for finding your way to moviemaking—as most of the early directors did—after living some years in the world and gaining knowledge of life outside show business.... What Wiseman finds ties in with one's own experience."

The setting for *Law and Order* (1969), a film that continues to enjoy excellent distribution, presented innumerable opportunities for Wiseman to "take sides." That he resisted these temptations reflects the sort of judiciousness that someone much younger might not have brought to the violence the film reveals.

"Whether he's recording volatile or placid incidents," wrote Gary Arnold in the *Washington Post,* "Wiseman looks at them without shame and without sentimentality."

More than most films, Wiseman's are wide open to differing interpretations. In the absence of clear authorial guidance, critics and those in the general audience are free to "recreate" the films: to supply motivations and produce small personal stories within Wiseman's larger one. With no narration to explain what is "really going on," no music to take the viewer's emotional hand, and in all but a few films (*The Store, Central Park,* and *Aspen*) black-and-white footage, the audience is offered an unparalleled do-it-yourself opportunity. For some, this poses a challenge, but Wiseman film enthusiasts say they can concentrate on what matters without the distractions of sound and camera razzle-dazzle, narration and music.

In *The Store* (1983), a Neiman-Marcus salesman spreads a fur jacket for a young prospective buyer to admire, remarking that sable is "a Texas fur." It is a rather bland scene in my judgment. But this is what one critic, Mary Lou Weisman (no relation to the filmmaker) saw and reported in *The New Republic:* "This is all ceremony and they both know it. The man is going to buy this sable jacket. It is a matter of honor. He has roped his first steer, had his first woman, found his first oil well, made his first million, bought his first Cadillac, and now he must do right by the missus. The bull paws the dirt, but the camera leaves the area before he charges."

As Wiseman has said on several occasions, "The only safe assumption to make about the public is that they're about as smart or dumb as I am. I can't anticipate how people are going to react. . . . My job is to make the best film I can and hope that what I've done will connect with other people's experience and interests."

Most critics report, in a relatively straightforward way, what they see, or think they see, in Wiseman's movies, and some (Pauline Kael, David Denby, Robert Coles, Frank Getlein, Tom Shales, Richard Schickle) have moved on to suggest what these things mean and how Wiseman achieves his effects. Few have failed to describe the films as "complex." And many have remarked upon their similarity to novels. Wiseman, himself, agrees with both observations.

In 1986 he made four films about people who were blind, deaf, or had multiple handicaps. The documentaries were shot at the Alabama Institute for the Deaf and Blind. Together they run nine hours. John O'Connor wrote in *The New York Times* that they would be an ideal choice for inclusion in a time capsule to be opened in a couple of hundred years, "for they would show our society at its most caring." The setting might suggest a clinical approach. But here, as elsewhere, reviewers like Robert Coles found Wiseman "a visual poet," arranging and composing reality "as artists or writers do," putting him in the company of Raymond Carver, Richard Ford, Toni Morrison, and others who are "storytellers, not social scientists."

Few contemporary filmmakers have so frequently been compared with writers. Pauline Kael was one of the first to do so in a 1969 review of *High School*: "[He] extends our understanding of our common life the way novelists used to..." she wrote. Here is David Denby on *Hospital* in *Atlantic Monthly* (1975): "The outward blandness is reminiscent of Hemingway, Orwell, and the Depression photographers." And Wiseman, himself: "I approach my [editing] just like someone writing a novel: the events are not staged, of course, but the way I condense and rearrange them is not the same as in real life. I call my work reality fiction.... There's no reason a documentary film should not be as complex and subtle as a good novel."

The comparison between writing and Wiseman's filmmaking is almost always linked to his editing. This is where most of the composing is accomplished. Wiseman talks of "internal" and "external" editing. The first is how he compresses an hour of real-time film into five minutes "to make the sequence appear that it took place in the way it's being shown." External editing, by contrast, is the way the individual, edited sequences are related to each other to make a structure for the film.

"Both," he explains, "are related, in large part, to the material" (i.e., what is being filmed). Here he notes that *Zoo* (1993) has a lot more cuts than *Juvenile Court* (1973), "because in *Zoo* at least half the participants didn't speak English very clearly and the pictures told the whole story, whereas in...*Juvenile Court,* what people say to each other is more important, and you have to allow time for them to say it...so that what they say is adequately comprehensible to someone who sees the film only one time."

The assembly requires time and patience. Wiseman uses only one foot of film for every twenty-five feet shot, and he usually spends at least eight months editing each film. He sees the editing as a mosaic process—piecing together individual cuts to make sequences that eventually create the whole film and, finally, the entire *oeuvre*.

Many have commented admiringly on Wiseman's technique. On October 1, 1973, Frank Getlein made some observations in the *Washington Star* that might apply to many of the films: "Generally, he doesn't cut within the scene. He stays with the person doing the talking, only occasionally—and often to great effect—panning across to others, a discernable, but not dominating editing rhythm—each large take is surrounded fore and aft by a series of short ones.

"By scattering his shots, he avoids the deadly lack of movement inherent in the form and . . . creates a continuous sense of the larger background within which individual confrontations are played out. This complex, effective technique is what makes Wiseman an . . . artist as well as an immensely informative feature journalist."

In a recent conversation, Wiseman told me, "I'm pleased that people refer to the literary quality of the films. I think it's because I reject the idea of simple, didactic, thesis-oriented films. I'm interested in complexity and ambiguity, not in simplifying the subject in the service of any particular ideology . . . I hope that when someone sees my movies he knows what my views are. But if I could summarize my views in twenty-five words or less, I shouldn't have made the movie, I should have written the twenty-five words."

Just as good books merit more than one reading, so many of Wiseman's films are worth a second look. This is because some of the remarkable things going on in them are obscured by the off-handedness of how they are presented. Take a couple of sequences from *Missile* (1987), a film about training Air Force officers to man the launch control centers for Minuteman missiles. In one scene we see a student making a mistake on a simple countdown. Later, a staff officer complains about a student who, during an exercise, launches a missile without authorization. "We are talking about a big error there, right? A three bagger . . . a critical error," he says to the class. A student asks, "Did he make it through the program?" and the instructor replies, "Barely."

Coles' reference to the Depression photographers is apt. There are, in nearly all Wiseman films, memorable, if fleeting, images that haunt viewers long after the entire movie has faded: wind and rain-battered outdoor advertising, an empty street, or face, or room. Such pictures bring to mind Edward Hopper's lonely people and places, Dorothea Lange's photograph of a pensive "Migrant Mother," Manet's painting of a bar girl at the Folies Bergere, staring at us intently but without comprehension.

○ ○ ○

Wiseman has made one of the greatest single contributions to noncommercial television since it was established in 1952. In part this is because of his talent as a skillful documentarian, an authentic artist, as his editing alone makes clear. Fortunately technique is matched by his choice of subjects. "I pick places," he says, "that are successful in their own terms, places with complex issues. It's too easy to shoot sitting ducks. You have to discard your simple-minded notions, otherwise you are doing propaganda." In such places, as Robert Coles has commented, "complexities, ambiguities, ironies, inconsistencies and contradictions" abound.

Wiseman has persistent regard for the people who inhabit these places, never masking or simplifying their nature. This attitude is difficult to maintain. It sometimes has the effect of making the familiar strange and the strange familiar. "If I start to dilute the material," he says, "that's a very patronizing attitude . . . horrible."

Much credit must also be given to his uncommon, single-minded, hard-working manner. This is infrequently a characteristic of what many call genius. "It is not an altogether easy job," wrote Michael Arlen in *The New Yorker* in 1980, "or a widely popular one, this stripping down, this rearranging of the old scale in order that we may hear new music, but . . . it is simple in the noblest sense, and brave, and by no means without love."

It is true that public TV has supported Wiseman's work rather grudgingly. Most of the support for his films has come from foundations—chiefly Ford, MacArthur, Aaron Diamond, and Joyce. (In 1982 Wiseman received one of the MacArthur Foundation's five-year "genius" awards.) But about 20 percent of the support for the films came from public broadcasting sources, according to his own analysis in the mid-1990s. On one occasion, when a CPB "peer group" review panel turned down Wiseman's request to make the Neiman-Marcus film, *The Store* (asking why he had not selected Gimbel's or Macy's), one of Wiseman's bureaucratic CPB nemeses, the director of programming, correctly reversed the decision.

WNET also served as "sponsoring station" for Wiseman films, putting up the money for film-to-tape transfer and publicity expenses, though nothing for production. Wiseman represents his relationship with WNET as a good but limited one: "They haven't created any obstacles for me."

Moreover, public television has provided Wiseman with his only access to a national TV audience and has extended that accessibility on his own terms—no editing. If Wiseman needed to rely upon the commercial networks for funding and exposure, he may have stopped making films many years ago.

Not only do Wiseman films provide an opportunity for today's Americans to observe their collective lives, but the documentaries also will be of immense value many decades from now. Public television was not established precisely to showcase incisive social commentaries, but it is useful to know that when given the chance to do this it responded positively, and has continued to do so steadfastly.

Most television material is highly ephemeral. It is therefore remarkable that someone with serious intent and talent chooses to devote most of his professional life to producing for TV a body of work in the way historians of the past, such as Toynbee, or novelists like Balzac and Dickens, created substantial work for personal and public libraries as well as contemporary consumption.

I asked Wiseman recently how such close encounters with so many and such different people have influenced his life. His answer: "I have increasing respect for the integrity and decency of most people most of the time, and an awareness of the complexities of intervening in people's lives. I have also developed a wariness of slick, easy, and simplistic solutions to complex problems."

Who we are, few would argue, determines what we notice and judge to be important. In this respect, public broadcasting can be grateful that Frederick Wiseman has been its leading film documentarian in its early decades.

He is now [February 1998] editing his thirty-first film. It will be completed in ten months. He says it is about a small town. That is probably all he will ever say about it. Everything else will be in the movie.

In the early 1950s Frank Baxter was a curiosity, a professor on television who lectured on Shakespeare in the same style he used in the classroom—as a reporter remarked, "without benefit of giveaways, girls, or gimmicks." *(Photo: Current Newspaper, from tape provided by Whalley & Associates, Long Beach, CA.)*

Before *Masterpiece Theatre* or *American Playhouse* there was *An Age of Kings*, Shakespeare's history plays in fifteen parts. At left: Julian Glover (in cape) plays Edward IV, late in the series. *(Photo: National Public Broadcasting Archives.)*

In the '60s, several stations in the noncommercial system enjoyed financial stability and production resources, but KQED was both the envy and pride of them all. Its success was due partly to its location. More important was its highly creative staff and the management styles of James Day, its first president (above, center), Program Director Jonathan Rice (above, right), and Richard Moore (left), who was hired as membership director and succeeded Day as KQED's president. *(Photo of Day and Rice: KQED; photo of Moore: Twin Cities Public Television.)*

On a trip to London, Stanford Calderwood (above, left) decided to make a "cold call" on the BBC to ask if they would like to sell programs to WGBH. The call set in motion the creation of what would become the most prestigious and enduring drama series in American public television's history— *Masterpiece Theatre*. The concept had also occurred to Christopher Sarson (above, right), who later became the first executive producer, and who chose the series' signature musical theme and selected Alistaire Cooke (right) as the series' host. *(Photo of Calderwood: © John Dillon; photo of Sarson: WGBH Archives; photo of Cooke: WGBH.)*

Upstairs, Downstairs was a phenomenal success both in Britain and the U.S. But when *Upstairs, Downstairs* was first screened for the Americans, Executive Producer Christopher Sarson balked. He thought it was a soap opera, unworthy of the WGBH series. *(Photo: WGBH)*

The eleven-part, thirteen-hour television series *Brideshead Revisited* was one of American public television's greatest hits. Even fans of WGBH's *Masterpiece Theatre* were unprepared for this astonishing tour de force, presented by the Boston station's rival, WNET in New York. Pictured at Castle Howard in Yorkshire, which supplied Waugh with his inspiration for Brideshead Castle, are Anthony Andrews (left) as Lord Sebastian Flyte, Diana Quick as Lady Julia Flyte, and Jeremy Irons as Charles Ryder. *(Photo: WNET)*

When Fred Rogers arrives in his neighborhood, singing his opening song and changing into his informal sweater and sneakers, he seems to be saying, "Now I'm all yours. This time is for you"—in most children's lives, rare behavior for an adult. *(Photo: Family Communications.)*

At his Steenbeck editing console, Fred Wiseman assembles and condenses sequences for one of his groundbreaking documentaries. *(Photo: © Margot Balboni.)*

One of Julia Child's greatest accomplishments is that, although manifestly far more capable than we are in a technical sense, she consistently reminds us of ourselves in our own kitchens, where life is frequently fraught with flops, hazards, and greedy opportunities masked as taste-testing. *(Photo: WGBH)*

More than two decades ago, Jim Lehrer and Robert MacNeil gave public television an entirely new kind of news program. *The Mac-Neil/Lehrer NewsHour*, now *The NewsHour with Jim Lehrer*, became one of public TV's leading series, and for many viewers it *is* public television. *(Photo: Don Perdue.)*

"Folks hate to be taught, but they love to learn"—Michael Ambrosino, the creator and original producer of NOVA. Above right, an artist's conception of what will happen when a really big asteroid hits Earth, from "The Doomsday Asteroid." *(Photos: WGBH)*

The American Experience needed a host, someone who could supply historical credibility and the continuity that many felt was absent. David Mc-Cullough is a historian and author whose work includes books on the Panama Canal, the Brooklyn Bridge, Theodore Roosevelt, and the Johnstown flood. *(Photo: Steve Behrens, Current Newspaper.)*

Judy Crichton was executive producer of *The American Experience* from its beginning until her retirement in 1997. She says, "I wanted to make films that had an on-going life. I think that if I'm proud of one thing that would be it." *(Photo: Steve Behrens, Current Newspaper.)*

Jessica Savitch (left) was *Frontline*'s series anchor throughout the first season. "If anybody had the ability to look into a camera," says David Fanning (below), *Frontline*'s executive producer, "and say, 'America, pay attention,' Jessica could do that. We didn't realize how much her star was in danger of disintegrating." *(Photo: WGBH.)*

12

Julia Child—The French Chef

The publication in 1998 of a seven-hundred-page, hugely detailed biography of Julia Child (*Appetite for Life—Julia Child,* by Noel Riley Fitch) has bestirred a Manhattan memory. One evening toward the end of the 1960s, my wife and I were having dinner in New York at La Caravel, a gracious French restaurant.

Dining there was a treat; the food was excellent and the service quietly efficient. The place held a special allure for me because it was the site of a superb documentary by Nell Cox, *French Lunch.* The short film records events in the kitchen from the first luncheon order through a frenetic, almost balletic crescendo of culinary movements at dinnertime—punctuated by the flare of flaming dishes—and finally subsides in a relaxed, post-service meal for the waiters and cooks themselves.

On this occasion we had arrived early and were watching the small inner dining room fill up with expensive-looking people anxious to eat and make their sprints for the theater, and others who had come to make a gustatory night of it. After we had ordered and the theater-goers began tucking into their meals, one large, adjacent banquette remained unoccupied. Then they arrived, a glamorous group of six or eight garrulous men and attractive women (memory seems to conjure up a sprinkling of Kennedys) dominated by a tall (six foot two, we all knew) smiling lady whose voice was once described by a TV critic as "a Boston accent with a touch of mashed potatoes." She was instantly recognizable as Julia Child.

The entire room was attentive, most especially the *maitre d'hotel* who was ecstatic. And why not? Here we were in the presence of the first major television-created personality in the cooking world, the successor to Fannie Farmer (another Bostonian), Irma Rombauer (*The Joy of Cooking*), and, one might almost say, the great Auguste Escoffier himself (after all, she had studied in Paris with one of Escoffier's most prominent students, Chef Max Bugnard).

This was the cook as star, WGBH's *French Chef*. This was the author of *Mastering the Art of French Cooking*, a book that had persuaded us that cooking was not a chore but an art, and could be a lot of fun as well. We all called her "Julia," though few of us had ever seen her in person.

The roomful of celebrity-watchers did their best to keep eyes discreetly averted, but there was a perceptible hush when Julia studied her menu and began to order.

Julia Child first came to the attention of WGBH, Boston, in 1961, when a friend of hers told an English professor from Boston College, P. Albert Berhamel, about a new cookbook and suggested he interview its author on his book program, *I've Been Reading*. A date was set, but before her scheduled appearance the station burned to the ground (on October 14, "the morning after Friday the 13th," people at Channel 2 still call it). According to an early station press release, her eventual TV conversation with Professor Berhamel in a makeshift studio was her gesture of commiseration.

All the same, it was characteristic of Julia's enterprise and good sense that she brought along, in addition to *Mastering the Art of French Cooking*, the ingredients for making an omelette, which she proceeded to do. She beat some egg whites in a large copper bowl with an equally large balloon whisk—implements not often found in American kitchens at that time.

The program staff had been talking about producing a cooking series and liked the liveliness of her on-camera appearance. Robert Larsen, then director of programs, invited her to outline a cooking series. According to David Ives, former president of the station, her summary was "so clear and thoughtful" that a decision was taken to produce three half-hour pilot programs in the summer of 1962. These were followed by a series of thirteen thirty-minute shows. By the time she was done, *The French Chef* totalled 119 programs.

The early programs were produced in the demonstration kitchen on the second floor of the Cambridge Power and Light Building—part industrial plant, part office—behind the smokestacks that lined the banks of the Charles River. The fire had destroyed everything at WGBH except the remote truck. Seven "studio sites" were hastily improvised in various parts of Boston while a new facility was constructed. The Power and Light Building on Blackstone Street was one of these. The place featured a freight and passenger elevator, one of those wire cages summoned by pushing a button, which set off a loud bell that could be heard throughout the building. In those early, nerve-wracking production days, most TV programs were rehearsed, then shot in their entirety without interruption, and recorded on kinescope with little or no editing.

David Davis, then a staff member, remembers sitting in the remote truck. "Julia was twenty minutes into her first show, and the elevator bell rang. I thought, 'What are you going to do?' She was whipping away at something [and] said, 'Oh, somebody's at the door, but I'm much too busy.'"

Russ Morash, who was producing the program, recalls her pausing, then saying, "Oh, that must be the plumber. About time he got here. He knows where to go." In any case, her talent for improvisation (which she emphasized in cooking as well as TV production) was early and clearly evident.

Much has been made of Julia's on-camera *faux pas*—flipping the potato pancake onto the stove by mistake, adding wine instead of oil to a dish, and reaching for a pound of butter and finding a note to the prop girl to put it there. They became part of her public persona. In fact, these errors were quite rare, for she was, and is, greatly meticulous in every aspect of organizing her programs. In the beginning, she spent nineteen hours preparing for a typical half-hour show, with a large number of people—most of them volunteers—assisting behind the scene. What people really recall were her recoveries from the rare mishaps, her cheerful off-handedness. In the case of the famous pancake flip-out she remarked, "But you can always pick it up," which she did, adding, "If you are alone in the kitchen, *whooooo* is going to see?" As she tipped up a wine bottle to drink what was left in its heel, she smiled and observed: "One of the benefits of being a cook." My personal favorites were her casual remarks, as when she poured a little wine into a dish and said insouciantly, "Never use water unless you have to."

One of Julia Child's greatest accomplishments is that, although manifestly far more capable in a technical sense, she consistently reminded us of ourselves in our own kitchens, where life is frequently fraught with flops, hazards, and greedy opportunities masked as taste-testing.

When her first program was about to be broadcast, Julia and Paul Child pulled a TV set from their fireplace, where it was kept, to watch *The French Chef,* as she wrote, "*lurch* onto Channel 2." Noel Fitch quotes an early critic who wrote, "Each program had about it the uncertainty of a reckless adventure." Still another journalist, commenting on the Julia Child style, said that the shows were "as impromptu as the practical improvisations of Fred Astaire."

Whatever the perception, nearly everyone agreed that she was in life what she seemed to be on TV. After an interview with the *Christian Science Monitor*'s TV critic (October 23, 1963), he wrote: "She is the only television personality I have ever known whose manner is the same off-camera as on."

The first *French Chef* (featuring boeuf bourguignon and French onion soup) was produced on January 25, 1963, and broadcast on Wednesday at 8 P.M., Feb. 11. WGBH repeated each program a week later at 3 P.M. (According to David Ives, repeats became so numerous that "for years there was hardly a day when she did not appear on Channel 2.")

Initially, four programs were produced each week, a punishing schedule, especially for Julia's husband, Paul, who lugged all the supplies to the kitchen and was present from the planning stages to the wash-up. They worked twelve-hour days and completed thirty-four programs in six months. Eventually, they cut back to three, then two, and, at the end of two years, they were making one program a week. In the process some spontaneity was lost to an increasing number of cue cards and the programs took on a more polished and professional style. Design research supplied the dining room set used in the final scene, the one in which Julia brings in the meal, lights the candles, raises her glass, and wishes everyone "Bon appetit."

Two hundred fan letters were received in the first twenty days. Soon four hundred letters were coming in each week. By the time *The French Chef* was distributed across the country by National Educational Television (predecessor to PBS), Julia Child had become a local legend, taking her place alongside Boston Pops conductor Arthur Fiedler, Paul Revere, and the Red Sox. Pressured as she must have been, Julia nonetheless found time to supply forty-five recipes and short essays on cooking to the *Boston Globe*—free.

National distribution of the new series, beginning in 1964, was one of a handful of program events in the early life of noncommercial TV that signaled the arrival of public television as an important dimension of American cultural life—something few would have suspected by reading NET's first press release about "a series of programs that show the techniques of French cooking." A year later, Julia won the prestigious George Foster Peabody Award for "distinguished service to television."

It should be recalled that in the early 1960s the leaders of educational television were quite ambivalent about providing any entertainment in programs—which *The French Chef* assuredly did.

From the start, the series was an unqualified success. *Newsweek* reported that it was "helping to turn Boston, the home of the bean and the cod, into the home of the brie and the coq." Ted Holmberg, writing in the *Providence Sunday Journal* observed, "I couldn't be less interested in cooking . . . but I can watch Miss (sic) Child prepare a leg of lamb . . . and remain fascinated for half an hour."

In San Francisco, where requests for her recipes were flooding into public TV station KQED at the rate of twenty thousand each week, the *Chronicle*'s Terence O'Flaherty called Julia "television's most reliable female discovery since Lassie." It was a broad audience, from "professors to policemen," said *TV Guide*.

About a third of the recipes used on the program were drawn from her newly published book, *Mastering the Art of French Cooking*. Requests for recipes were so overwhelming that NET needed to send out instructions to all stations, limiting the number of replies. By August 1963, less than a year after *Mastering* came out, Alfred A. Knopf had sold one hundred thousand copies at ten dollars a copy. It seemed destined to become a classic. In 1966 the Childs took nineteen thousand dollars from the *Mastering* royalties and built a small house in Provence, where they spent six months each year for the next twenty years. (A second volume of *Mastering* was published in 1968.) There was a certain irony in this, for Knopf published it only grudgingly after Avis DeVoto—wife of Bernard DeVoto—intervened on Julia's behalf. By 1998, she was working on her tenth book.

WGBH paid Julia and Paul Child fifty dollars per program in the early days. By 1966, this was increased to two hundred dollars plus expenses. In addition to her undoubted loyalty to the young public TV station, it could not have escaped Julia's attention that her popular TV cooking demonstrations would greatly enhance book sales. But this was only part of her relationship with WGBH and public television in a larger sense. She had an aversion to making her work commercial.

In the fall of 1964 she addressed a food journalists' conference, donating her five-hundred-dollar fee to WGBH. It was something she did frequently. As she told a reporter for *The Nation's Business,* "As long as I can get clothes and a decent car, I'm not really interested in the money end of it."

The money end of cooking on television had not been neglected by food companies. When local commercial TV stations came on the air, many home economics teachers—resembling nurses in white uniforms—were recruited to talk about food groups, how to save household money and how to bake cakes. However, few were found who could cut the mustard, so to say. James Beard, a truly gifted and enthusiastic cook, was unsuccessful on TV. Dione Lukas, who operated a restaurant in New York, was far more popular and appeared often from 1948 to 1953. Poppy Cannon ("the can-opener queen") enjoyed a good run as a regular on CBS's *The Home Show.* Betty Furness played to a more up-scale market and was commercially ubiquitous.

In 1964, Olivetti offered Julia $2,500 for her photo with a typewriter, but she turned it down. (Paul Child often referred to the "Madison Avenue hounds.") However entertaining her programs may have been, she considered herself an educator, not a performer. As Noel Fitch writes, "She represented public television; she believed she could never endorse a product, nor accept money to represent a profitmaking institution." This stand lent credibility, both to WGBH and to her own opinions. (Julia was one of the first, but by no means last, to take this position. Many years later, NPR commentator Daniel Schorr was offered more than $1 million dollars to be a "spokesman" for Avis Rent-a-Car. He refused, saying, "I have spent fifty years building the reputation I have, and the first time I was on the air with this, I would throw away that reputation.")

She participated in the station's Christmas party skits and hosted holiday parties for the staff at her Cambridge home (much better attended, according to some, than the station celebrations). On one of these occasions she and her producer, Russ Morash, worked up an interview in which he asked her questions about how the Boston Symphony programs were edited. Her demonstrated answers included chopping up two-inch videotape with one of her meat cleavers.

Although she consistently turned away all commercial blandishments, her work on TV did prove considerably rewarding for others, perhaps none more than her Boston butcher, Jack Savenor, who displayed a newspaper picture of her taped to his scales. "How many geese do you think a guy could sell in a year?" asked Savenor. "Maybe six, maybe seven. But the week after she works on the goose, I sell sixty-five." Julia herself was a good customer. For her first near-Christmas program in 1963 ("How to truss, stuff, brown, roast, braise, sauce, and carve your goose") she required four geese: one raw, one slightly cooked, one fully roasted, and a spare.

Another Boston merchant phoned WGBH the morning after Julia demonstrated how to clean a fish. "I've had twenty-four knives for cleaning fish in stock for years, and this morning I sold every one ten minutes after I opened." Copper bowls and balloon whisks were nearly impossible to find soon after the series began its national run. As *Time* reported, "When she cooked broccoli, the vegetable was sold out within two hundred miles of the broadcast station."

Julia McWilliams Child was born Aug. 19, 1912, and was, she has said, "an adolescent until I was thirty." One of her grandfathers left Illinois in 1849 when he was sixteen to pan for gold in California. Her mother, tall and lively like Julia, had roots in New England. Julia grew up in Pasadena in a large house with drivers, gardeners, cooks, and a kitchen that both she and her mother rarely saw or cared about. She played center for her private-school basketball team and enrolled in Smith College where she lived what she describes as a "butterfly life," driving her friends around in a Ford and graduating in 1934.

When the nation entered World War II, she went to Washington as a "government girl," joining the Office of Strategic Services (the OSS, predecessor to the CIA), where she hoped to become a spy. Instead she was sent to Ceylon as manager of a typing pool. Here she met Paul Cushing Child, an artist-turned-OSS-mapmaker, and her future husband. Both were further assigned to China where Paul's intense interest in food—and growing interest in her—became manifest.

"I decided to seduce him by learning to cook," Julia has written, "so [after the war] I went to cooking classes back in Beverly Hills." They were married in 1946. Paul died in 1994, at age ninety.

Paul Child was a world-class dilettante: a former lumberjack, teacher, linguist, talented gardener, and polo player, he was also an excellent artist and photographer, a writer (for the *Boston Globe*), and sometime poet, who wrote sonnets with meticulous metric structure for his wife. Following his OSS stint, he joined the U.S. Foreign Service. Eventually the Childs were posted to Paris where he was exhibits officer at the U.S. Embassy. There his gourmet proclivities had their greatest effect upon

Julia, who began studies at what was arguably the world's finest school for cooks, the Cordon Bleu. "Our class began at seven in the morning," she says, "lasting until eleven. Then I went home and cooked a magnificent lunch for my husband. In the morning the students cooked, supervised by their teachers. But in the afternoon there were demonstrations conducted like an operating theater, with chef and stoves, the audience banked up in front of him. I immediately adopted the towel at the belt, now so much a part of me in the kitchen I cannot cook without it." She reports that at this time "my main difficulty was not in learning how to cook, but learning how to eat sensibly."

Julia remained at Cordon Bleu for six months. About this time, she met Simone ("Simca") Beck and Louisette Bertholle, who later joined her in organizing a successful cooking school of their own, L'Ecole Des Trois Gourmands. With these colleagues she also embarked upon research for *Mastering the Art of French Cooking,* a ten-year project. Always a perfectionist, she believed each recipe had to be tested several times by different people. "A cookbook is only as good as its poorest recipe," she would say later.

When Paul was assigned to Marseilles and later to Oslo, Washington, and Philadelphia, Julia opened a "branch" of her school in each new location. Paul retired from the State Department in 1960 and the couple moved to a three-story clapboard house in Cambridge, where John Kenneth Galbraith and Julia's TV producer-to-be, Russ Morash, were neighbors.

"We live in a lovely town, because everyone is doing something," she said at the time. Speaking of the friends from Harvard, WGBH, and Boston's publishing interests, she remarked, "We encountered each other as people whose heads were always above the crowd." (This was physically true of Galbraith, who was nearly seven feet tall. Marion Schlesinger—wife of Arthur Schlesinger, Jr.—referred to Galbraith and Julia as the "benign storks" of her neighborhood.)

In these early Cambridge days, her biographer tells us, Julia was a heavy smoker—even between courses. This stopped when she required a mastectomy in 1968. There was another cancer scare two years later.

We are also told that she wished to be called "Mrs. Child," that she "loved gossip, talking dirty, a good belly laugh," and that she has had two facelifts. (Julia has said that the biography makes it sound as if she were dead.) The biographer, Ms. Fitch, reports a friend of Julia remarking that the reason she won't consider retirement is that she's afraid that if she retires she will die, and that she is afraid of death. A more likely reason for her aversion to retirement might be the one she passed along to Frank Prial of *The New York Times* in the fall of 1997: "Retired people are boring."

After moving to Cambridge, Paul became his wife's agent, road manager (they traveled widely to publicize the new book) and sometime dishwasher.

David Ives was assistant general manager of WGBH when *The French Chef* was first produced and knew both Paul and Julia. "He was a difficult guy to get to know—kind of aloof," says Ives. "He was very bright and had high standards. You got the impression he was doing this because he was enthusiastic about Julia, but that it was not what he himself would have chosen. He was very inventive. He and Julia had a small station wagon, and he attached a large slotted cooking spoon to the radio antenna, so if you were driving around town and saw a slotted spoon passing by, you knew it was *The French Chef*." Describing Julia, Ives believes her to be more complicated than she sometimes appears. "She's really dedicated to what she does and has a tremendous inner drive to accomplish things."

In 1970, when Julia's programs began to be distributed by PBS, they finally appeared in color. "I'm really sick of black and white food," she told a journalist at the time. Her work with producer Russ Morash (and his wife, Marion, who became an accomplished cook herself, and one of Julia's regular assistants) extended into the 1980s with three additional series, *Julia Child and Company, Julia Child and More Company,* and *Dinner at Julia's.*

The WGBH programs were followed by *Cooking with Master Chefs, In Julia's Kitchen with Master Chefs, Baking with Julia,* and three *Cooking in Concert* pledge specials, all produced for PBS distribution by A La Carte

Productions and Maryland PTV. In March 1998, at eighty-five, she embarked upon what she vowed would be her final series—*Julia Child & Jacques Pepin: Cooking at Home,* in which she returns to demonstrating cooking basics in her own kitchen, with her friend Pepin.

Henry Becton, now president of WGBH, came to the station immediately after graduating from Harvard Law School in 1970 and has observed Julia in all seasons, often appearing with her at fundraising events and celebrations. "One of her chief characteristics is endurance," he says. "In social situations, especially dinners in her honor, I would be collapsing when she was just hitting her stride."

"It's a shame," Julia has said, "to be caught up in something that does not absolutely make you tremble with joy."

Many have spoken of Julia's "generosity as a teacher." Becton, pressed to define the chief reason for her success, speaks of her as "greatly empowering—she made people feel they could do what she did." She told her viewers: "If I can make a souffle rise, so can you." Millions did. And I am happy to be among them.

On that long-past evening in New York, when the hush fell over La Caravel's dining room, I listened intently while Julia chose from the menu precisely what I had ordered a few minutes earlier. A coincidence, of course, but I was thrilled; a taste, perhaps, of becoming empowered.

13

Talking with Jim Lehrer

In 1970, on a steaming summer morning in Dallas, I walked into a large room of the public TV station KERA and met Jim Lehrer for the first time. He was seated alone at the end of a long rectangular table, its surface strewn with daily papers, reporters' notes, overflowing ashtrays and half-empty mugs of coffee. He was studying a clutch of wire service stories, shirt sleeves rolled back, tie pulled away from his unbuttoned collar—the city editor from central casting, I remember thinking.

In fact he had *been* a city editor—of the *Dallas Times Herald*—only a few months before. Now he had a new position, director of news and public affairs at KERA, where he had quickly become the producer of *Newsroom,* a nightly, hour-long program in which local journalists reported and commented on the day's events.

Over the next twenty-seven years we talked by phone a few times and occasionally exchanged short notes. Now and then I would see him on his way to or from a Washington party and kid him about my continuing preference for the format of *Newsroom* over that of his present program. He would smile indulgently.

Then, on a crisp autumn day in 1997 I went out to WETA/Washington to meet with him again. The documentaries and coverage of the Watergate hearings were behind him, his close, twenty-year association with Robert MacNeil had ended (some forty-five hundred programs and fifteen thousand guests by 1994), and he had been going it alone since 1995. He had suffered a coronary and heart surgery in 1983, and mod-

141

erated the presidential debates in 1996. Along the way, he had written fourteen novels and three plays. There were children and grandchildren. Some of all this was mirrored in his face, more rumpled now than his clothes had been in Dallas. His forthright manner hadn't changed, however, nor the Texas way of dropping his "g's" when he starts tellin' stories.

James Charles Lehrer was born in 1934 in Wichita, Kansas. By the time he reached KERA he had been a reporter and editor for ten years (for the *Dallas Morning News,* as well as the *Times Herald*), had spent three years as an infantry officer in the Marine Corps and had received undergraduate degrees from Victoria College (halfway between Houston and Corpus Christi on the Gulf Coast) and the School of Journalism at the University of Missouri. He had seen a lot of Kansas, moving from Wichita to Sedrick to Marian to Independence, while his father, a second generation German immigrant, ran a small bus line. He and his brother then moved with their parents to Texas, eventually to Dallas.

"I'm not a religious person," says Lehrer. "My grandfather on my mother's side was a big church person—one of the founders of the Nazarene Church. I have uncles who are preachers, and my brother is a Baptist minister. But my mother revolted against all that. I was not raised in a religious environment. So I believe in religion, but I'm personally not religious, and I'm troubled by it." He grew up in a musical family where his mother played the piano, and an aunt and uncle were professional musicians. But this, too, seems to have left no lasting impression. Today he regards music largely as "background stuff." It was his mother who helped steer him toward literature and writing, pursuits that continue to occupy much of his attention. He speaks about his father with the intensity, one might say fervor, of a filial true believer: "He was the most moral person I ever knew. He really believed you didn't cheat, didn't lie, you *always* told the truth. He taught my brother and me those old-fashioned things in ways that were terrifying. I grew up thinking that if I *did* do any of those things, somebody would...

"He wasn't mean, just the contrary. He taught us to believe those things were important. If someone gave him too much change, he'd hunt him down and return the money. He thought that individually we all had to be good. If we were, there would be no problems, no need for cops."

In a story Lehrer tells, he and his proud parents are guests at a reception for *Viva Max,* a film with Peter Ustinov, adapted from Lehrer's first novel. The drinks are liberal and everyone is in high spirits. Near the end, his father, a little tipsy, rushes over to him, grips his arm and says excitedly, "Godamighty, Jim, I just told somebody *I* wrote *Viva Max!*"

Growing up in Kansas, some of the people he remembers best were teachers who "put a lot of stock in words and stories." But in those days a far more serious interest was sports: "I wanted to be a baseball player, to play for the Dodgers ... doesn't everybody?"

His attention turned to journalism when he was about sixteen and living in Beaumont, Texas, where his father was managing a bus depot. "I wrote a paper on Dickens' *A Tale of Two Cities* and my teacher commented on the margin 'You write really well, Jimmy.' This happened about the time I was coming to grips with the fact that I probably wasn't going to make it as a professional athlete."

Instead, he made friends with some of the reporters who came to the ball games and determined to become a sports writer. This led to reading short stories and to "a really good English teacher" in San Antonio, where the family had moved. She introduced him to Hemingway and other authors as he became editor of the newspapers in high school and then Victoria College. After graduation, in 1956, from the University of Missouri's School of Journalism (from which he later received its medal of honor— the most meaningful, he believes, among dozens of subsequent recognitions), he embarked upon a three-year hitch in the Marines.

Like other men whose military experience left deep and lasting impressions (often persons who thrived in the system and whose lives were further enhanced), there is a seriousness underlying Lehrer's descriptions of life in the service, even in the jokes and light-hearted anecdotes.

"I went from white buck shoes and no responsibilities to a mud hole, responsible for forty guys, some of them older than me. It was a maturing experience. The Marine Corps taught me all sorts of things: how to get people to move from here to there, how to get them to understand what you're saying. In the Marine Corps you look somebody straight in the eye and say, 'This is *it*. This is the way it *is*.' You know there's no bullshit about it.

"In the Marines you learn to talk in people's context. If I say something to a PFC that is totally out of his frame of reference, I've wasted his time and it could cost him his life. You learn to *communicate*. I think it helped me later on."

(Later in our talk, and on a totally different subject, Lehrer used the same tone in describing how he had held the attention of an important guest while the studio ceiling caught fire, by fixing him with his eyes, not allowing him to look up until the live segment was completed.)

"The bottom line is: I came out of the Marines knowing what I could do. I didn't have to be a he-man, to prove myself. I'd already done that. It freed me up. I also learned my limits. The Marine Corps pushes you to your limits. Psychologically and physically, it's wonderful to have that behind me."

After the Marines, and for the next ten years in Dallas, he was a newsman, working twelve hours a day and writing fiction in some of the time left over. "It was exhilarating," he says, "but terribly hard work."

Near the end of this period, in 1969, Mark Carliner, a young man with slender production resources and a strong desire to make a movie adaptation of *Viva Max,* offered Lehrer an unusual deal: the producer would pay him a percentage of the *budget* (up to fifty thousand dollars) in exchange for free film rights. The movie was made and, after paying his agent, Lehrer walked away from the *Times Herald* with forty-five thousand dollars, intending to write fiction full-time.

It didn't last long. Almost immediately Robert Wilson, head of KERA, phoned with an offer to become the station's part-time director of news. His first assignment was to apply for a Ford Foundation grant to establish a nightly news program based on a successful format initiated two years earlier by public TV station KQED in San Francisco.

KQED had hastily conceived the daily *Newsroom* format (originally *Newspaper of the Air*) during the first weekend of a city-wide newspaper strike. The station hired reporters off the picket lines and assigned stories that they presented and discussed informally on air with other news people. It proved to be immensely popular, even after the two-month strike was settled. By this time the programs had attracted national attention. Fred Friendly, former CBS News president and then an advisor to the Ford Foundation, persuaded the philanthropy to make a $750,000 grant to KQED for a continuation of the series and, more important, to offer similar support to other public TV stations willing to make a *Newsroom* commitment. Stations in Dallas, Washington, and Pittsburgh took the challenge.

Lehrer flew to San Francisco to observe the program and talk with Friendly. Some seed money was raised in Dallas, Lehrer's proposal to the Ford Foundation was successful, and *Newsroom* was soon underway with Lehrer (who had no previous TV experience) as its producer-editor-moderator.

It would be difficult to overstate *Newsroom's* influence on public and commercial TV. Dozens of similar local and national variations on the series were soon set in motion, many going strong thirty years later, as *The McLaughlin Group* and *Washington Week in Review* demonstrate.

In 1973, Lehrer received a fellowship from the relatively new CPB. "It was one of the best things that ever happened to me," he says. "The awards were set up for people . . . from other lines of work, who could then be drawn into the public system." In Lehrer's case, it meant attending a lot of conferences where he learned the history of public broadcasting and was invited to join the fledgling PBS as coordinator for public affairs. He also became an on-air commentator for a public affairs production unit, National Public Affairs Center for Television (NPACT), run by newsman Jim Karayan. Here Lehrer met Robert ("Robin") MacNeil, a Canadian who had been a foreign correspondent for Reuters and a reporter for NBC and CBC as well as a documentary film producer for the BBC. As it happens, they had both been in Dallas reporting President Kennedy's assassination but had never met until they began to produce documentaries on social issues for NPACT, broadcast by PBS.

◇ ◇ ◇

In mid-May of 1973 the Senate Select Committee on Watergate opened its hearings and, as Lehrer says, "For the next four months we sat bun to bun, reporting the events in prime time." It was a critical period in the personal and professional lives of both journalists, and a reporting event that moved educational TV to public television.

"A lot of people [in public TV] thought it was a lousy idea," Lehrer remembers. He credits Gerry Slater, then head of public affairs for PBS, with engineering a commitment to the Watergate programs from the major public stations—in Washington, New York, Boston, Chicago, and Los Angeles, then gaining acceptance from the others.

"MacNeil and I were aware that this was new ground for public TV," Lehrer recalls. "We were on *every night*. This is the first time anyone had used prime time in a public affairs way. It was a *huge* thing, and we knew it."

They came away convinced that a nightly public TV news program was needed, and doable, but not under Jim Karayan's direction. "He was in a different world," says Lehrer. "It was a daily fight to do what we did. We decided we wanted to do it our way. Arrogant, but there it was."

The Watergate hearings also forged a personal bond between MacNeil and Lehrer unique in broadcasting journalism, where egos are large, fuses often short, and competition hot. Lehrer recalls feeling provincial at first and intimidated by MacNeil's extensive experience: "He was a foreign correspondent, he'd worn out eight or nine trench coats. I'd been in Nuevo Laredo and that's about it." But it soon developed that they lived in the same Washington suburb (Bethesda), and their daughters attended the same kindergarten. Near the end of a co-anchor career that spanned two decades, they were talking to each other on a private phone line ten or twenty times each day. MacNeil was present every day following Lehrer's heart surgery, and there were long talks between them when MacNeil's second marriage began to fall apart. The bond now extends into the hereafter, as each has named the other as guardian of his children.

"My friendship with him," Lehrer told writer John Grossman in 1994, "has made it possible for me to live a full and fruitful life. It is a vital part of what my life has been these last many years."

Once asked whether there had not been any small but persistent irritations in this unusual relationship, Lehrer's response was quick and characteristic: "It wouldn't have worked if we'd had an ongoing disagreement. And it would have been a pain in the ass."

After Watergate, MacNeil went back to the BBC, returning two years later to commence *The Robert MacNeil Report,* an evening half-hour, single-subject news program produced by WNET in New York. That was September 1975. Lehrer first appeared on the program two or three times a week as its Washington correspondent. In six months it became *The MacNeil/Lehrer Report.*

"The best aspect of that format," Lehrer reflects, "was our commitment to one story for thirty minutes. The downside was our lack of flexibility. It sometimes got very ponderous. As MacNeil has always said, 'It takes a lot of courage to be boring.'"

After eight years, a decision was made to extend to a full hour, starting in 1983. It was not easy or, in Lehrer's words, "That was from hell. We went from thirty minutes on a Friday to an hour the next Monday, from a *supplement* [to network news] to a *replacement.* We made a lot of mistakes, . . . bad calls . . . it was a terrible agony."

Technical problems were daunting and easily matched by the uncertainties—and, in some cases, strong opposition—of public TV station managers. "It was a close call," says Lehrer. "We almost didn't get renewed. Had we been in commercial TV, we would never have been allowed to screw it up, then correct it."

Renewal of the PBS contract for the *MacNeil/Lehrer NewsHour* came, in fact, on an extremely close vote of local stations. "The politics of the system nearly destroyed us," says Lehrer. "People had their axes to grind; they wanted to cut us back or replace us with their own programs. But we won, we survived, by a small margin."

Al Vecchione, producer of both the half and the hour-long programs, remembers that it was "a considerable leap without much of a safety net. We were giving up a very successful program that we'd had going for seven years."

Lester Crystal left NBC, where he had been producer of the *Nightly*

News and president of the network's news division, to become the *NewsHour's* executive producer. "We assembled," he says, "what I think was a very talented group . . . but we hadn't worked together . . . and despite all the experience, when you do a project like this, you sometimes don't know how it's going to work until you get on the air, and that's what happened to us."

Part of what happened was that three months into the new series (and two minutes after he had been on the air live) Lehrer had a heart attack and went directly to the hospital for triple bypass surgery.

The experience frightened both news anchors: "It certainly straightened him out in a hurry," MacNeil mused afterwards. "He was a guy who would drive to the corner, one block, to buy a couple of packages of cigarettes . . . and eat pastrami sandwiches with mayonnaise for lunch everyday."

Judy Woodruff was recruited from NBC to pinch-hit for three months while Lehrer recovered. It was a trying time that Lehrer later described in his book *My Heart, Your Heart.*

During the next twelve years the *MacNeil/Lehrer NewsHour* became one of public TV's leading series. Due to the highly selective nature of much noncommercial television viewing, for many it was public television. By 1995, the program claimed seventeen million viewers weekly, of whom 63 percent said they would believe the *NewsHour* above all other TV news services. Satellites began carrying the program to Europe, Asia, and Africa.

Still, it was not an altogether smooth ride. The ever-restive and often querulous local station managers grumbled, as did some viewers. The most often heard criticism—judging from Lehrer and MacNeil responses—was that the program was boring and the mini-debates between well-chosen guests were too predictable.

When the "boring" charge came up in a (1995) program marking MacNeil's departure from the series, both partners expressed indignation: "The people who watch it all the time don't find it boring or they wouldn't watch it," huffed MacNeil. "This medium is driven increasingly by the tyranny of the popular."

Lehrer seemed equally put upon: "You pay taxes or you're on Medicare, if you're a young person who may have to go to a foreign shore with a weapon in his hand, that ain't dull!"

Both were especially sensitive to any complaints that the program was not sufficiently interesting. During the trial of O.J. Simpson, for instance, some said the program had not given enough coverage to that major media event. Lehrer's reply, after explaining that the *NewsHour* had covered the important news of the trial, was "We're not in the interesting business, we're in the importance business."

Meanwhile, viewer loyalty remained undiminished even as the anchors mounted some pretty high horses to defend the series. When, on his last program, MacNeil thanked the audience for "understanding what we do," many were probably nodding their agreement.

And for good reason. While it may be taken for granted now, in 1983 a full-hour news TV program in prime time was a surprising and welcome innovation. In the years that followed, the series quietly introduced a wide variety of segments new to programs of this kind, including political stump speeches (on the theory that few people at home get to hear a real campaign speech anymore), a weekly two-person political analysis (now Mark Shields and Paul Gigot), frequent essays, and extended interviews with influential people. In the early days, Lehrer recalls, *NewsHour* reporters needed to spend fifteen minutes telling prospective interview subjects what public TV was and another fifteen explaining the program. Not anymore. "Now we more often than not get the people we want when we want them," says Lehrer.

Although he routinely interviews heads of state and socializes among some of the rich and famous, he appears not greatly impressed with these associations. Soon after Princess Diana's death, Katherine Graham, chairman of the board of the Washington Post Co., wrote "an appreciation" in which she recalled hosting a small dinner party for the Princess who was considering what to do with her life. Jim Lehrer, also a guest, observed that she must have "stacks of invitations." She agreed, but added, "I've got to decide." Whereupon Lehrer said, characteristically, "Make sure it matters to you. Because if it doesn't, you cannot make it matter to others."

While Lehrer's professional loyalties and interests are in journalism, what matters to him is writing fiction. Now working on his fifteenth novel, he has also written three plays. MacNeil, whose first ambition was to be a playwright and actor, also wrote books (*The Story of English* and fiction) while he coanchored the *NewsHour.* When asked why, MacNeil replied, "Because television is not enough."

Lehrer agrees: "If all I had to make my mark was television, maybe I wouldn't be [satisfied] just asking questions. Maybe I'd want people to get up from their TV sets saying, 'Boy, old Lehrer gave him hell!' If I didn't have my writing, maybe I wouldn't be so comfortable. It's a maybe, but I know this: when I get up from my [on-air] chair, I have other ways to have my say. And I have my say. When I sit in my living room with a full shelf of books I've written...I think it's healthy to know that what I'm doing [on the program] tonight is not where I have to take my stand, stake my claim. When I was seventeen I decided I wanted to write fiction and become a newsman. Hemingway said, 'You do your journalism, you make your mark writing fiction.'"

Today Lehrer reads a wide variety of fiction including spy novels (a genre he has explored in his own books), watches public TV's *Mystery!* series, some sports, but very little news or public affairs.

In 1994 Lehrer knew that his partner was thinking of leaving the program. Then one day MacNeil simply said, "I don't want to do this anymore."

"I knew it was coming," says Lehrer. "But would he stay one or two more years?" This was an important question at the time, for if MacNeil left in 1995, Lehrer would have had full responsibility for the following year's presidential election coverage.

Soon after that, a Friday, the Lehrers took an overnight train from Washington to visit the MacNeils at their house in Connecticut. The plan was to spend the weekend discussing MacNeil's departure. Lehrer told his wife, Kate, he planned to open the subject right away, no small talk. The MacNeils met them at the train and before anyone had finished orange juice, Lehrer said, "Well, look, let's start talking. One or two years?"

"Jim, it's going to be one year," MacNeil replied.

To which Lehrer responded, "Oh (expletive)! What do you mean?"

The weekend was spent ironing out details. They made two lists, one containing their goals, and the second how to achieve them. The largest problem was closing the *NewsHour*'s New York production center at WNET, where the first program had been created. Now the work of *The NewsHour with Jim Lehrer* would be consolidated at WETA in Washington.

"It was difficult on many levels," Lehrer says. "For twenty years, MacNeil and I were always together. On judgment calls there were two heads. We trusted and respected each other and agreed often enough to make it work. I had to figure out a way to replace him. I had decided that if it didn't work out, I would walk, too. I didn't want to develop another unique arrangement, not at this stage of my life. The other thing was, I had to replace Robin in my life."

In the end, subanchors were brought in, there would be a lot more people on the air, and the editorial decision-making process would change. In earlier days, the staff members made their suggestions and final decisions were taken by, as Lehrer says, "god-one" (MacNeil) and "god-two" (himself). Now the daily 10:15 A.M. senior staff meetings and the once-a-week advance planning sessions would be more democratic. In the past, Lehrer admits, MacNeil was inclined to slow the process and ask for second thoughts. Part of his own impatience, Lehrer believes, was rooted in his experience as a city editor: "Somebody would come up with an idea, and I would say yes or no before he finished. Now I've begun to listen. I have to."

Listening is something he frequently mentions in discussing his work on the air: "The No. 1 skill is to be able to listen, under fire. Anybody can write questions, but if you haven't developed the ability to listen to the answers . . . you'll never make it."

Talking with Jim Lehrer at his Dallas Newsoom table in 1970 and twenty-seven years later in his Washington office were not altogether different experiences. On both occasions he was direct, friendly, and self-assured; then and now a man who knows more clearly than many what he wants and how to get it. At sixty-three, he is more avuncular, and over the years the Texas accent has moved to the fringe of his speech. Happily, his voice never resembled the more sophisticated tones of Robert MacNeil. But anyone who thinks his plain-spoken manner reveals a down-home provincialism would be greatly mistaken.

After two years, *The NewsHour* with Jim Lehrer seems to have found the format that suits its featured anchor and executive editor. He says he doesn't watch the recorded program after the broadcast as much as in the past, but is still frustrated when he doesn't get the words just right, doesn't follow up properly, or gets too wordy. "If you don't have those kinds of anxieties, the adrenalin doesn't flow properly. I know the potential for screwing it up is there every night. The way to avoid that is to pay attention."

He talks of the future with the same equanimity that he brings to reflections on the past: "I just want to keep writing my books, and want this program to continue to get better. But that's it. I'm not waiting for that magic moment. I know I'm the most fortunate person I've ever come across. I've been able to do the things I've wanted to do—and I'm still doin' them. I'm enjoying the hell out of it. I've got a wonderful family, a great life. Talk about *boring!*"

14

Wall $treet Week's Louis Rukeyser: One for the Money

One evening in London, in 1966, Anne Darlington, a Johns Hopkins graduate on a Fulbright Fellowship, was surprised to see Louis Rukeyser, then chief of ABC's London bureau, on a BBC interview program. She remembered him as a writer for her hometown newspapers, the *Baltimore Evening Sun* and the *Sun*. Four years later, in January 1970, Darlington was preparing a TV series on sports fishing for the fledgling Maryland Center for Public Broadcasting when someone at a Baltimore cocktail party suggested that a series on economics and financial management might be more appropriate. One of the Center's executives scribbled the idea on a piece of paper and gave it to Darlington, adding, "Do you think you can do anything with this?" She thought she could.

"By summer," she says, "I had it plotted, knew how many programs, the format, the budget. How to make people watch it was the difficult part. It needed a host who knew more about economics than TV." Then she remembered the BBC program . . . and Rukeyser. By this time he had moved to New York as ABC's chief economics correspondent, the first network newsman to hold that assignment.

"Once I got Louis in my head," Darlington continues, "I couldn't get him out. I interviewed some others but they wouldn't do. Louis knew both economics and TV. I finally got up my nerve to call him. And, God bless us and save us, he answered his own phone! I was tongue-tied."

She asked for his advice, for names of those he thought could host a financial program. He said he'd give it some thought. The following week she was more forthright, saying only he could make it fly. He was intrigued but skeptical, especially about how it would affect his network connection.

"I said to Elmer Lower, the president of ABC," Rukeyser remembers, "I can get my Friday commentary taped on Thursday. I go down and do this little PBS show for thirty weeks.... You won't lose anything, and you might get some brownie points with the FCC. They agreed to it. Then, of course, the tail began wagging the dog." He left *ABC News* in 1973 as his career broadened, and the thirty-week commitment to *W$W* became, by 1998, a nearly thirty-year engagement.

"I had the panelists, the set had been designed, Louis was the last piece of the puzzle," says Darlington. The first *Wall $treet Week* program, subtitled "Who's the Average Investor?" with special guest Stan West, research director of the New York Stock Exchange, was broadcast on November 20, 1970. It also featured a Baltimore banker and an insurance executive, B. Carter Randall and Frank Cappiello, who both became regular panelists. Rukeyser's style was evident from the beginning as he pleasantly but firmly pressed a reluctant Mr. West to tell the audience whether brokers give a brush-off to the little guy who wants to sell less than one hundred shares.

The program was greeted three days later by Jack Gould's *New York Times* review under the headline, "Little TV Station in Maryland Looks at Wall Street." "Who would have thought," mused Gould, "that the financial press would have some rivalry from Channel 67 atop a Maryland hill?" Who, indeed? In its twenty-eighth year, *Wall $treet Week* with Louis Rukeyser still reports that it is watched by more people than read the *Wall Street Journal* and by more than watch any other TV business program.

In its first year the series treated basic issues such as: "What Makes a Successful Investor?" "What to Expect from Common Stock Investing?" "How to Make Money in Mutual Funds," and "What Women Should Know about Managing Their Money."

"In the second year," Darlington says, "we began branching out." While the programs' content may have been widening, their form was taking a shape that would remain remarkably unchanged through the years. Writing in *Investment Vision* eight years ago, Richard Levine describes the programs "as ritualized as Kabuki drama, as strictly choreographed as 'Swan Lake.'" As part of the ritual Levine included the ten technical analysts who Rukeyser named "the Elves" with their up, down, and neutral predictions, as well as Rukeyser's own "puns, his patented wink and grin."

It seems altogether probable that Rukeyser's Friday evening pavane within the setting that Darlington hoped would "resemble a boardroom cum penthouse" is more than a small part of the program's hold upon its loyal audience, calming the viewers through constancy and continuity, soothing as a familiar fairytale, confirming the steadfastness of the financial community. Its buy-and-hold philosophy of program presentation reassures nervous investors as it informs and entertains them. *W$W* benefits from the allure of an ever-changing investment market combined with a predictable program format—a *Mister Rukeyser's Neighborhood* for grown-ups.

On the Friday after "Black Monday"—October 19, 1987, when the market lost 508 points—Rukeyser's first words were, "It's just your money, not your life." He abandoned his regular format and talked throughout with three guests. As if to prove that ritual would not be broken, the producers subsequently folded the altered format into the series, and it has become a "regular change" approximately every three months. Another ritualized break is the annual "New Year's party" (gentlemen in black tie) during which they check predictions against the market's actual performance.

The program's Elves have their own weekly prediction ritual as well, which has become fair game for comment by financial journalists who compete with Rukeyser. In July, *Mutual Funds* magazine observed that stock analysts were expecting a bearish period in the market because the "Elves" featured by Rukeyser were *bullish* seven-to-one. Indeed, stock prices tumbled late the next month. The three previous occasions when the Elves showed a "plus-six" split, in March 1991, January 1992, and May 1996, also preceded "protracted periods of market drift or outright correction," according to the magazine. W$W publicist Caroline Lewis replies that the Elves' predictions are more accurate than Mr. Fosback's.

One of the most unusual fixtures of W$W's formal structure since the start is the receptionist ("Ms. Smythe" as she is known to the production crew), who escorts Rukeyser to a place among his panelists and appears to mingle, if somewhat stiffly, among the guests at the program's close.

"At the start," Darlington explains, "the programs were live, and we needed someone who could walk on and off to straighten out any on-camera technical emergency. Louis' mike was on a long cord that could become entangled in the furniture. A man would have been too distracting. The audience would say, 'What is *he* doing?' Natalie Seltz [who served in the role] was a TV director and knew technical matters. She could walk around the set unobtrusively." Seltz was the first of several "Ms. Smythes," and has now returned to the role.

Another reason for "Ms. Smythe's" presence was (and one assumes still is) to act as a "minder" for special guests who, Darlington says, "might have great reputations but were deathly afraid of looking foolish on TV. So 'Miss Smythe' met them, talked to them, calmed them down."

During W$W's first year there was an abundance of panelists and guests. Darlington remembers spending two or three days in New York interviewing them: "I like to know *exactly* what I'm getting," she says, "face to face." In the second year the panelists were cut back to seven or eight, and she began to put Carter Randall and Frank Cappiello on together each week. The panel since has grown to twenty-six, who take turns on-air, including analysts who follow special sectors of the market.

The formula worked almost too well, it seems, for her small staff—Darlington, a project assistant, a part-time secretary, and a part-time researcher. They received more than two thousand pieces of mail in the first year, and sixty-six thousand pieces by year three.

Soon after the program began to appear locally and on eleven stations of the Eastern Educational Television Network—including New York, Philadelphia, Pittsburgh, Baltimore, and Boston—the search for its continuing financial support began. The budget for the thirty original half-hour programs was $108,602, of which the newly established CPB contributed $85,000. Rukeyser himself earned $10,200, or $300 a program, according to one Maryland PTV budget from this period. (He remembers his fee as two hundred dollars per program.)

Today, the program—now produced jointly by MPT and Rukeyser Television, Inc.—appears on more than three hundred stations, behind only a few series such as *Sesame Street* and *This Old House,* and its budget has grown to $2.8 million for fifty-two episodes. Rukeyser today does not discuss his salary, but an experienced budget-watcher at PBS guesses that he earns about $300,000 a year.

Within a few months of the program's premiere, national public broadcasting officials were anticipating its popularity—and worrying about FCC problems with its underwriting. CPB's head of programming, John Witherspoon, asked consultant Thad Holt to help raise money for the show, but warned that it "might run afoul of [public TV's] underwriting policy in the course of a very worthwhile effort."

The field then was very sensitive about accepting financial support from sources that might influence, or appear to influence, program content. Public broadcasting executives and funding specialists joined in an extended ethical struggle that tried the patience of nearly everyone involved.

Here is Jeremy Wintersteen, a CPB fundraising advisor, writing an August 20, 1971 memo for his own records: "First blush confidence for finding corporate underwriting for [W$W] wanes somewhat when one considers the arm-length situation and the understandably skittish financial public relations' stance of publicly held corporations. Stock brokerage firms are obviously out."

Perhaps at first. But the FCC's and public broadcasters' comfort with corporate underwriting grew considerably over the years. In 1998, W$W was supported by grants from Prudential Securities, Inc., A.G. Edwards and Sons, Inc., and Oppenheimer Funds, Inc.

Following W$W's appearance on PBS, *The New York Times* modified its reception from surprise to cautious optimism, John O'Connor concluding that the program "doesn't provide the complete solution to the prob-

lem of presenting economics on television. But it comes close and is determined to get closer." In 1980 the *Times* ran a long Sunday feature on
W$W, ending: "Almost every year there are efforts to produce imitations,
yet almost none are successful."

Anne Darlington left W$W in the late '70s to oversee the production
of all MPT programs. She was succeeded by her assistant, John Davis,
who now hosts and produces Maryland PTV's *Motorweek*. Rich Dubroff,
now the executive producer, has been producing the series since 1981.

Throughout W$W's history Louis Rukeyser has never stepped out of
its spotlight. "Louis saw its potential immediately," says Darlington, now
an independent media and political consultant. "He never once said it
wouldn't work, as many people did." In addition to his presence on
more than thirteen hundred programs with nearly a thousand guests,
Rukeyser has greatly influenced the program's format and style.

"We had a brilliant but erratic first director," recalls Rukeyser. "He
had the idea to open each show differently—camera placement, the way
the set looked, and so on. You had some arty shots in which I couldn't
find the camera and the audience didn't know what the hell was happening. I finally said to him, 'Look, Johnny Carson comes out every
night, five nights a week, stands in the same spot, in front of the same
curtain, and people never say, what a boring shot. They say Johnny was,
or wasn't, funny tonight.'"

He attributes the program's shape and content to viewer response.
And to this, Rukeyser says, he is "extremely attentive," reading all the
comments, favorable and critical, each week. "The program's structure,"
he says, "is designed to be fail-safe, the guest occupying only about a
third of the total time. I've heard every conceivable comment about the
show over twenty-eight years—except 'You had the wrong guest
tonight.'" Guest-driven programs are far more common in television.
This one, intentionally, has balance.

"In the beginning there was no concept that the opening commentary would be such an important part of the program. [But] it was perfectly clear from the early days that what was catching the audience
was that opening." Rukeyser, who says he thinks of himself first and

foremost as a writer, composes his four- to five-minute program introductions about two hours before the program opens. "I write every syl-
lable," he says. "When people want to be kind, they say 'please tell your
writers not to give you that material.'" Kevin Anderson of *USA Today*
once asked Rukeyser whether he ever experienced writer's block in
those last moments before the show. His response: "I was chief rewrite
man for the *Baltimore Evening Sun* when it had nine editions a day. You
learn to get unblocked." Like many successful TV hosts, Rukeyser
claims never to think of his audience of multi-millions. As he explained
to *New York Times* writer Neil Reisner in 1980, "I am talking to one person, whom I regard as intelligent, with a good sense of humor but not
all that technically knowledgeable."

The program's panelists are given specific audience questions in advance. "Otherwise," says Rukeyser, "they might not know and give the
wrong answers. Then where would we be?" The special guest segment,
admired by financial professionals and laymen alike, has included Alan
Greenspan, Ross Perot, Paul Volcker, John Kenneth Galbraith, Malcolm
Forbes, and Paul Samuelson. One of Rukeyser's chief regrets is that he
has not (yet) hosted a sitting President.

Other guests are eager to come, however. "When you're in financial
markets, getting on this show is what everyone dreams of," Paine Webber executive Andrew Shore recently told *Fortune* magazine.

Louis Rukeyser was born on January 30, 1933, the second of four sons
of Merryle Rukeyser who had become financial editor of the *New York
Tribune* at twenty-three and wrote a column for International News Service for three decades. His older brother, "Bud" (Merryle, Jr.), now in
retirement, was an executive vice president and top spokesman at
NBC. William was managing editor of *Money* magazine, then *Fortune*.
The fourth brother, Robert, was an IBM executive before becoming senior vice president for Fortune Brands ("The only one in the family with
a legitimate job," says Rukeyser).

Merryle Rukeyser, Sr., appeared on W$W on several occasions, first
when he was eighty-seven and in the year he died at nearly ninety-two.

Rukeyser says he remembers two pieces of parental advice: get into a business where you can exploit the labors of others, and one where you can regularly take capital gains. He later told his father he realized with mortification that he never took the advice, but consoled himself that his father never did either.

"All I wanted to be when I grew up," recalled Rukeyser recently, "was a newspaperman—now, of course, a sexist title. I worked for [the *New Rochelle Standard Star*] as a school correspondent when I was eleven. I was paid as a sports reporter when I was sixteen, and I've been a professional journalist for half a century."

He graduated from New Rochelle High School, where Rick Breitenfeld, later head of MPT when *W$W* began, was a class ahead of him. Rukeyser remembers Breitenfeld acting extremely deferential in their first days at MPT—until Breitenfeld learned that brother "Bud" was the Rukeyser a year ahead of him, not Louis as he had mistakenly thought. (Breitenfeld has recently retired as president of WHYY in Philadelphia.)

At Princeton he enrolled in the Woodrow Wilson School of Public and International Affairs and its Public Aspects of Business program, was president of the Press Club (although he took no courses in journalism), covered University news for several metropolitan newspapers, and graduated in 1954, determined not to follow his father into economic journalism. He started as a fifty-five-dollar-a-week reporter for the *Baltimore Evening Sun* and became the chief political correspondent (at age twenty-four), head of its London bureau, and its Asian correspondent in India, winning two Overseas Press Club prizes. In that period he also enlisted in the U.S. Army and served two years in West Germany, working for the Army newspaper, *Stars and Stripes.* In 1965 he joined ABC News, first as its Paris correspondent, then head of its London bureau and later, economics commentator.

"Wherever I went in the world," says Rukeyser, "it was perfectly obvious to anybody with an IQ over 62 that the worst covered subject in journalism is economics. The typical journalist not only knew no economics but was proud rather than apologetic about it. In my newspaper and ABC days I found myself the only one doing those [economics] stories. On the one side you have the Washington people who have no concept of what's going on, and on the other the financial junkies who aren't quite sure who Newt Gingrich is. I've always thought that the area that needed coverage was the largely unchartered frontier where politics and economics overlap."

During his much-traveled life Rukeyser has acquired a wide variety of cultural experiences, including a more than passing acquaintance with good food and wine. "When I die," he says, "just scatter my ashes over La Domaine Romané Conti"—one of the smallest and most prestigious vineyards in France. Early in life he determined to eat in each of the Michelin three-star restaurants in France before he was thirty—a promise he kept.

A man once described by *People* magazine as "the dismal science's only sex symbol," Rukeyser for some years has appeared on published best-dressed lists and once did a walk-on in a feature film, *Big Business,* during which Bette Midler knocks him to the pavement and steals his taxi. (He subsequently told an interviewer that the cameo appearance was "worth a little more in lecture fees, but nothing as a human being.")

Married to a former British journalist, Alexandra Gill, he is the father of three grown daughters and lives on four acres in Greenwich, Connecticut ("back-country Greenwich," he insists, "with well-water and septic tanks").

Gambling has been a serious hobby—"a relaxation," as he puts it. "I love it. I've gambled all over the world," he enjoys saying, "from Monte Carlo to Monaco to Estoril." He's no high roller, however, and he professes not to confuse gambling with investing. "I confess that I enjoy it less than I once did, because these days it's difficult for me to be at a blackjack table for more than twenty minutes before a half dozen people have said—as if it were the funniest line of the century—'Ah, you find this a better bet than Wall Street, do ya?'"

Years ago, his brother Bill, then managing editor of *Money* magazine, urged him to review six books. He refused, until he learned they all concerned gambling. "Once you have read the literature," he says now, "there's nothing to discuss at a blackjack table. If you just play sensibly, you can improve your chances of escaping with your life."

Lecturing and conducting large "investment conferences" has consumed much of Rukeyser's time. For years he gave as many as eighty talks (always on the same topic, "What's Ahead for the Economy?") between September and June. He is one of America's highest paid public speakers. For seventeen years, beginning in 1976, he wrote a column on economics that appeared in three hundred newspapers (for the first five years, three times a week).

In 1992 he switched to newsletters: first *Louis Rukeyser's Wall Street* and two years later, *Louis Rukeyser's Mutual Funds.* He revels in the newsletters' combined 400,000 circulation ("the runaway success of the decade"). Between the columns, the newsletters, lectures, and his *W$W* commitment, he has managed to publish three books: *What's Ahead for the Economy?, How to Make Money on Wall Street,* and, most recently, *Louis Rukeyser's Book of Lists—The Best, the Worst and the Funniest from the World of Business, Finance and Politics.*

"I can't do more than thirty lectures now without cloning," an expression he has used to describe his heavy schedule for many years. "Unfortunately, raising the fee doesn't seem to work," he adds. Not a man given to self-deprecation or deferential demeanor except to make a joke, his remarks about his life and prodigious professional accomplishments are often amusing and obliquely self-admiring. In conversation Rukeyser is affable, confident, and businesslike, not unlike his TV persona. The *W$W* press kit bristles with descriptions of the program's host. Although many appear to have been lifted from a high school yearbook, they are drawn largely from press accounts: "warm," "caring," "broadcasting dynamo," "best loved," "most trusted," and so forth. The latest description forwarded by his publicists was bestowed recently by the Museum of American Financial History: "Hero of Wall Street."

Rukeyser's image is carefully guarded by a publicist and assistants he describes as "a little jittery." One wary staffer, instructing me to send a letter requesting an interview, solemnly advised that I was not to neglect spelling the program's title with a dollar sign for the "S."

Rukeyser seems altogether at ease with his busy and financially comfortable life. "We believe in treating the acquisitive instinct with neither scorn nor reverence," he wrote in 1974. He might, as he subsequently made clear in a conversation, have become considerably wealthier than he is today. "I could have been rich beyond the dreams of anyone short of Bill Gates," he said recently, "if I had taken even ten percent of the commercial offers I've received." He tells the story of an agent for a "reputable American corporation" who offered him "a million dollars a year going in," and more, to become a corporate spokesman, and he could continue all his other professional activities. "[I said] I'm very flattered, their offer is very generous, but I think they want to buy what they would instantly cost me." Commenting on such offers Rukeyser says, "I think there's a difference between journalists and pitchmen . . . and cheerleaders."

More than a few people have expressed surprise that Rukeyser has not taken his broadcasting operation from Maryland PTV's suburban Baltimore site to a larger public TV station or a commercial network. He says he has refused many offers from commercial networks through the years. The way Rukeyser tells it, these temptations were predicted by Rick Breitenfeld soon after the program's early success. Breitenfeld told his new star that Rukeyser would "probably take the program to New York now that it's a hit."

"I told him," says Rukeyser, "if you'll look at my career you'll see that disloyalty is not one of my worst faults." It also seems plausible that his outspoken comments might find a less hospitable home in a commercial setting.

Though he didn't join a commercial network, Rukeyser continues to earn the largest TV rating in business reporting. For the 1997–98 season, the program had an average rating of 1.7 percent and a weekly "cume" of 1.898 million households, according to PBS Research.

(Public television also has the business-news show with the second highest rating—the nearly twenty-year-old *Nightly Business Report,* with an average rating of 1.0 percent last fall, according to *NBR*. Its weekly "cume" of 3.23 million unduplicated households is even larger than W$W's because the show appears five times a week.)

Wall $treet Week's ratings nevertheless are lower than often reported

(*Fortune* last month said it had a weekly audience of 4.35 million in-
dividuals, and the *Christian Science Monitor* in July gave a figure of 4.7
million households—more than twice what PBS reports), and the
numbers have declined as competition has grown. Its average audience is down from 2.05 million households in 1991–92 to 1.898 million last season, according to PBS.

W$W finds itself swimming in a crowded stream of business infor-
mation, with more than forty business programs appearing on broadcast and cable channels, according to a recent count by the Monitor,
and online investment data scrolling constantly across the computer
screens of many business executives.

I once watched W$W faithfully, but with so many other information
sources wheedling for attention, I've cut back my own viewing of the
show. And most of a small sampling of acquaintances—brokers, investment advisors, economic columnists—said that they watched the
program infrequently because it didn't provide information they did
not already possess.

"When I began *Wall $treet Week*," says its host, "people thought I was
nuts. They said the subject is just too dull or complicated. The average
American is intensely interested in money, if you can explain it to him
clearly and without putting him to sleep. People are more aware that
maybe they're not going to be Bill Gates, but they have to build a little
financial security for themselves."

In a 1978 interview with the *Los Angeles Times,* Rukeyser ruefully remarked, "It used to be when I was asked what made the show go, I'd
say it was because we were first in a field of one."

Now, offering a calm and pun-filled assessment of the business world
every Friday evening, he may find consolation in the fact that he is first
in a much larger field, one he has done much to create.

15

Inventing NOVA

On the first of May in 1971, Michael Ambrosino sat at his desk at 25 Wetherby Gardens in London writing a six-page, single-spaced letter to Michael Rice, vice president for programs at WGBH, Boston.

"This project in science," he wrote, "would begin to fill an appalling gap in PBS service. It would attempt to explain and relate science to a public that must be aware of its impact.

"The strand would be broad enough to cover all of science and . . . beyond its normal confines . . . biology, chemistry, physics, astrophysics, sociology, psychology, medicine, anthropology could all provide program topics."

The letter, filled with detailed explanations of production team schedules, content of programs, coordination with the BBC, and financial requirements, is a remarkably accurate description of *NOVA*, the series that Ambrosino named and ushered onto the air March 3, 1974. Even more remarkably, the 1971 plan still resembles what has become, twenty-five years later, the longest-running documentary series in America.

When Ambrosino proposed the series, he was on leave from WGBH and near the end of a year-long fellowship provided by the Corporation for Public Broadcasting (CPB). The fellowship had sent him to work with the BBC and to observe its production procedures. He was forty and an experienced producer. In 1957 he had joined WGBH, where one of his first producer-director assignments was *The Ends of the Earth— Explorations of Antarctica.* Two years later he was producing a series entitled *Science Six*, featuring elementary science experiments. In the '60s he produced, directed, and conducted TV interviews for programs that ranged from politics and election coverage to discussions of sex and drugs and music performance. By 1969 he was producer of *Michael Ambrosino's Show*, described by WGBH as "a cultural magazine that aims at putting Boston viewers in first-hand contact with their city."

In London he observed the BBC's Features Group and a production unit that was creating a strand of diverse, internationally acclaimed documentaries under the title *Horizon*. (Writing to Rice, Ambrosino described a "strand" as "a continuous run of broadcasts that a [BBC] unit presents and administers. Some are freshly produced, some are coproduced, some purchased and some repeated. This method allows flexibility, lowers costs, increases quality, enhances communications with foreign broadcasters, and spreads the responsibility of administration.") *NOVA* became the first of many WGBH strands.

Horizon had been established by a talented and extremely energetic program executive, Aubrey Singer (who later served briefly as the BBC's deputy director general). The *Horizon* unit had been formed within the new BBC-2 channel in the early 1960s. It soon attracted prestigious film producers who were given considerable independence in making single-subject, all-on-film documentaries.

Viewer reception to these programs—many rooted in scientific exploration—surprised everyone, not least the BBC itself. According to John Mansfield, *NOVA*'s fifth executive producer, "When BBC-2 arrived, it was agreed that science with a capital "S" must be given a special chance. There was little hope that it would be popular, but it was generally agreed that a dose of science television would do the country good." From the beginning, *Horizon* programs—such as "The Making of a Natural History Film," which later led off the *NOVA* series—were popular in the U.K. and throughout the world. For many years they set the standard for TV documentaries, winning every international prize available. When Ambrosino left England in the fall of 1971 he was determined to establish an American version of *Horizon* at WGBH.

In a "welcome back" press release in mid-September, the station described its delight at the prospect of resuming *Michael Ambrosino's Show* and, almost as a footnote: "In addition, he is working on the design of a project to make WGBH a major source of science programming on PBS."

Ambrosino could not have urged the creation of *NOVA* on a more receptive program executive than Michael Rice, who was familiar with the U.K. from his days as a Rhodes scholar and could appreciate the value of strong program ties to the BBC. Rice, who died at age forty-seven in 1989, is still regarded as one of the most intelligent and creative program managers in public broadcasting's short history. When Ambrosino went to England to begin his fellowship, Rice was immersed in choosing the first BBC dramatic productions for what would become *Masterpiece Theatre*.

"I never thought of *NOVA* as a science series," said Ambrosino recently. "I wanted to examine how the world worked, to use the scientific process of discovery as a narrative device to tell good stories. . . . We also wanted to use some of the talented scientists that were all around, at Harvard, MIT, and along Route 128 [Boston's high-tech corridor]. This was going to be an *active* series. We had very few limits on what we could or should do."

A long list of what Ambrosino calls "worthy" titles for the series was drawn up, including the public relations department favorite, "Eureka!" In the end he selected the title himself. "A supernova is something big, bright, new and bold, something to which you had to pay attention," he explained.

As fundraising began, he was frequently reminded of another and equally accurate description of a nova, i.e., making a big splash but then burning out quickly. "It was our little joke on the way public TV was funded in those days," says Ambrosino. "You could find money to start things but after a year or two the funders wanted to put their money into the *next* new thing, and your series would be left out in the cold and dark."

While he had hoped for a 1972 start, most agreed that finding the required funds (to say nothing of producing and acquiring programs) for a beginning in March 1974 represented a considerable achievement. In addition to a development grant from the American Association for the Advancement of Science (AAAS), the newly established WGBH Science Program Group found first-season support from the Carnegie Corporation of New York, CPB, the National Science Foundation (NSF), and the Polaroid Corp.

In his initial proposal, Ambrosino had projected a budget of $1,178,000 for thirty hour-long programs—twelve of them would be WGBH productions, four coproductions, eight acquisitions, and six rebroadcasts. The budget earmarked $60,000 for a group editor and staff, and $100,000 for publicity. In the end, the first season's thirteen programs cost about $1.5 million. By the third season the budget had doubled. (By contrast, NOVA's recent seasons—twenty new hour-long programs a year—cost between $10 million and $12 million. As Alan Ritsko, NOVA's managing director, explains, "About ten of these are original productions. Most of the others are mini-coproductions that NOVA controls from start to completion, sharing ownership and distribution rights with its coproducers.")

Fortunately for purposes of recruiting a skilled production staff, NSF and Polaroid committed funding for two seasons. When the word went out that there would be openings for three production teams, Ambrosino received 170 resumes. Interviews were conducted in New York, London, Los Angeles, and Boston. Robert Reid, former head of the Science and Features Department of BBC, became NOVA's chief consultant. Not surprisingly the three production team leaders were British, two of whom had worked for the BBC. One of them, John Angier, subsequently became NOVA's second executive producer. Many who helped produce some of the early programs became major producers at WGBH and elsewhere—including Paula Apsell, NOVA's present executive producer.

The teams eventually moved into new quarters at 475 Western Avenue overlooking the Charles River. Channel 2's new film facility, with its nine editing rooms, a small studio, and a viewing room, also was home of two other WGBH series, The Advocates and Religious America. Before NOVA had aired its first program, an additional production team was added to the Ambrosino's responsibility. Its assignment was to produce a lengthy program on death and dying in America, funded by a grant from the National Endowment for the Humanities (NEH). The program was produced and directed by Michael Roemer; he was assisted by David Grubin, who later produced film portraits of Presidents Roosevelt (Theodore and Franklin), Truman, and Johnson for the *American Experience* series.

By December 1973, Team One, under Simon Campbell-Jones, had completed "Where Did the Colorado Go?"—an examination of water management in the Southwest. It was the series' first original production and the second program aired. Angier and his team were finishing "The Search for Life" (origins of life on Earth), while former *Horizon* producer Francis Gladstone was in the midst of an ambitious dramatized version of the discovery of anesthesia, featuring Boston doctors in the leading roles. The series premier program, "The Making of a Natural History Film," was an extraordinary film-within-a-film *tour de force,* demonstrating techniques used by the Oxford scientific film laboratory, a production organization making nature sequences for the BBC. The first season also included programs on dolphin intelligence, nomadic tribes in the Amazon, bird navigation, nuclear fusion, and chimps learning sign language.

Such disparate subjects, a hallmark of *NOVA* from the start, have in common an emphasis upon beginning-middle-and-end stories. Storytelling was a major theme in Ambrosino's initial proposal to Rice, his subsequent memoranda to PBS stations, and his recent responses to my questions about his work.

"Producers are a naturally curious lot," he says, "and good documentaries are made out of that curiosity. They hear a new idea from a scientist, read a journal, attend a lecture, and 'bang,' they want to find out more. The topic chooses *you.* We were after good stories that could be told visually, and good storytellers. Some shows were assigned but most of the ideas came from the producers themselves. I just had to make sure the season had a flow and variety."

From the start, Ambrosino promised the stations that "science will be interpreted in its broadest context." Still, there were to be three areas of major interest: "basic science, science and technology's effect on society, and science's impact on public policy."

"*NOVA* will aim at having audiences feel: 'I can understand how science works. I can make sense of the world. I have an insight I didn't have before.'"

Both storytelling and drama informed most of *NOVA*'s programs in the first years, as they had influenced Ambrosino's early life. Born in Brooklyn, his family settled in Westhampton Beach on Long Island when he began high school in 1945. His father managed upper-income grocery stores in New York and owned his own specialty food store in Westhampton. "I took advanced math in a class of four," he recalls, "and physics with seven. There were twenty-eight in our graduating class." He played drums in a jazz band and was an enthusiastic member of the school's "spectacular drama club." At fifteen he was a dance band drummer: "I think I played every bar, senior prom, and Polish hall on eastern Long Island." With four others he also played in a volunteer fire department band, the Sons of the Beach.

He was accepted at Syracuse University to study physics, but switched to drama on the day of registration. "It was very romantic," he says now. "The only rep company on the East Coast, the Brattle Theatre in Harvard Square, went belly-up that same year." Still, he worked three seasons in summer stock. When he returned to Syracuse for a masters of science degree, after a hitch in the army overseas, he began to make TV programs. "In starting *NOVA*, I finally put my two loves [drama and science] together. I was lucky to find a road for my interests."

Ambrosino says he believes in "preparing for the accidents of life." An important one occurred in 1956 when he was invited to talk about closed circuit TV in the schools at a Harvard conference. (He had had six months experience.) Hartford Gunn, then president of WGBH, happened to be there. "Three weeks later," says Ambrosino, I was working at WGBH, developing school television for the State of Massachusetts. I was prepared. But it was an accident.

"Sitting at the next desk was the smartest and prettiest radio producer I had ever met. Lillian and I were married a year later and had three children." The Ambrosinos were married for almost forty years until Lillian's death from cancer in 1995. In addition to producing radio programs, Lillian Ambrosino was a reporter, one of the four founding members of Action for Children's Television, a government consultant in Washington and a lawyer whose clients numbered many independent film producers.

"Making good films and making them on time and on budget is tough," Ambrosino reflected recently. "We began production in '73 and there were few folks in Boston or the U.S. who knew [how to do it]. The series premiered in the spring of '74 with thirteen programs, and we returned with seventeen more in the fall. That's a killer pace, but I knew we had only one chance to take our message to the stations for [production funds] in the Station Program Cooperative, and I wanted us to survive."

In 1972 and 1973, each *NOVA* team spent seven to nine weeks on research. Much was done in the field, as the one-page outline grew into a full film treatment. The camera and sound crew then joined the team for four weeks of shooting—traveling about the country by plane, car, truck, and helicopter. This was followed by two months of editing by some team members while others began again on a new topic. As Ambrosino wrote in a memorandum to stations in 1976, "As with all science, the end of one story is the beginning of another."

"I think the producer's job is to find the power *within* the content, to have it grow out of the meat of the subject, not added on like sugar. All the pretty music and helicopter zooms [can't replace] finding that small seed and building a story around it.

"We tried to have the narration lag the awareness. Hopefully, the viewer will put the answer together just before the narrator's golden tones give it all away. In this way, the viewers are empowered and will seek out more on their own. That really is the task of public broadcasting, to set the audience out on its own search. The viewers are then on the road to self-education for the rest of their lives. Folks hate to be taught, but they love to learn."

The first thirteen programs were, of course, all new to the audience. In the next season, *NOVA* presented twenty-two programs, of which five were repeats. In 1976, there were twenty-six programs, of which six were repeats.

During these years, the *NOVA* staff worried about fulfilling its promise of basic science and science-related public policy—an objective never fully resolved. Popular programs about sleep and the sense of smell—great crowd-pleasers—tended to nudge out "important issues."

Worries over the proper balance of programs—and *NOVA's* general direction—have continued. In a paper reprinted in *Current* in 1992, Paula Apsell, then and now executive producer of *NOVA*, describes her concern, in 1990, for the series' diminishing audience and her reappraisal of program content.

"More than 250 past programs were divided into four categories and the average Nielsen rating was computed for each category," she wrote. Some of what they learned surprised the staff: "Challenging programs did not seem much of a deterrent to viewers," Apsell reported, "clearly the decisive factor was topic choice."

Topic preference groups were ranked from "death and destruction" (most popular) to pop-science (e.g., ESP and UFOs) to "bones and bodies" (dinosaurs and origins) to "boys and their toys" (aviation and military technology).

"Slowly and cautiously, we began to rethink the way we commissioned and scheduled programs... developing a wider variety of storytelling devices to match the broad array of content. After two years we have reversed the erosion of ratings and we are building audience."

Of *NOVA's* first fifty programs, nineteen were made by WGBH, nine coproduced, and twenty-seven acquired through purchase. The number of original productions had advanced annually from four to six to eight. The operation had been partly based, of course, upon the advantages of cooperation with the BBC and other production sources. The number of WGBH productions represented 36 percent of the total. It was more than the station had ever attempted or completed before. As Ambrosino noted ruefully in his third-season report: "As hard as it is, raising money is still easier than making good programs about serious subjects. Although we had more U.S. productions than we promised, it was still less than we hoped. *NOVAs* are hard to make."

In the first three years *NOVA*'s staff looked at 150 foreign-produced documentaries to purchase twenty-two. They were drawn from four BBC documentary series, from the British companies Yorkshire TV and Granada, and producers in Sweden, Yugoslavia, Switzerland, Germany, and Canada. A mid-'70s screening session in London confirmed that fewer British films would be on the market as the country's economic pressures increased—further reason to explore the tentative contacts that had been made with the Australian Broadcasting Corp., which eventually became a major source of program material. Ambrosino's objective of developing long-term relations with producers outside the U.S. was taking shape. It would prove to be an immensely valuable asset to *NOVA*, to WGBH, and to U.S. public television at large.

Three treatments were evaluated in these days for every program that *NOVA* agreed to coproduce. In some cases cooperation was largely financial. But in any case it meant more broadcast rights, a cheaper price and, frequently, considerable influence upon a program's direction.

NOVA opened its first PBS season on March 3, 1974, with, for those days, considerable advance publicity. Journalistic response was cordial: enthusiasm tempered by a certain dignity—perhaps befitting the scientific nature of the programs as the news media saw them. *Time* called attention to *NOVA* "filling the gap between deadly-dull 'educational' lecturing and pop-science trivia." Many papers, such as Portland's *Oregonian* were content with references to "high production values with intellectual curiosity," and the like.

Some national publications, *TV Guide* among them, dodged the problem of writing critiques of what apparently seemed esoteric subjects by hiring writers such as Carl Sagan and Isaac Asimov to create essays. Sagan wrote about "Life on Mars" in May, when PBS carried *NOVA*'s "The Search for Life on Earth." Asimov constructed an essay on chimpanzees ("They're smart but not smart enough") to supplement *NOVA*'s

program on attempts to teach primates to communicate. *Variety,* after a
nod to "some magnificent . . . breathtaking film moments," took the it's-
good-for-you approach: "All with an interest in science should watch
your TV schedule for *NOVA.*" Of one thing in its review of *NOVA*'s first
program *Variety* was entirely accurate: "With its scope, *NOVA* should be
good for seasons to come."

Most programs in the initial season seemed to offer journalists more
opportunities for rather bland and graceful acceptance than energetic
response. One exception was the program "Strange Sleep," a drama describing the discovery of anesthesia. It brought the *Boston Globe* to full
alert with a piece headlined, "Boston doctors star in Ch. 2 medical film."

Despite tepid reviews *NOVA* found its audience. And it grew. At the
end of the third season, the Nielsen rating service reported a national
average of 2.8 million households, and an audience range of four to
seven million viewers for each program.

"I left *NOVA* [after three seasons] in exhaustion," says Ambrosino. "I
never anticipated leaving WGBH for good."

John Angier became *NOVA*'s new executive producer while Ambrosino began designing a new series—*Odyssey,* twenty-seven programs
with an emphasis upon anthropology and archeology that was aired on
PBS in 1980–81.

Having raised the funds for *Odyssey* (from the National Endowment
for the Humanities), Ambrosino offered to bring it into WGBH. But the
station rejected his stipulation that he control the hiring and firing of personnel and the publicity, so he established his own nonprofit production
company, Public Broadcasting Associates (PBA), to produce the new series. As Ambrosino describes it, "We built a kitchen right in the center of
our production company and never had staff meetings. We just ate together. I put in a shower for the joggers, and we all got healthier and
could create an entirely different mood for work and play on the job."

Two-thirds of the *Odyssey* programs were made by PBA. After two
years, the company was ready to seek support, as *NOVA* had, through
the Station Program Cooperative. But the Reagan Administration had

cut federal funding for public broadcasting by 40 percent and the stations reduced their cooperative purchasing proportionately. Ironically, *Odyssey* was forced to compete directly with *NOVA* and, as Ambrosino explains, "*Odyssey* went down in flames."

Henry Hampton, president of Blackside, Inc., and producer of the two celebrated *Eyes on the Prize* series, a history of the civil rights movement in America, is one of Ambrosino's closest friends. They share a love of flying and for years have co-owned a plane, a Beechcraft Sierra. After *Odyssey,* Ambrosino worked closely with Hampton on all aspects of *Eyes on the Prize,* as consulting executive producer. "*Eyes* is one of my proudest credits," he says. "*NOVA* was important but *Eyes* was essential."

This was followed in the mid-'80s by *The Ring of Truth,* concerning the nature of scientific evidence. These were made with Phillip Morrison, perhaps America's most famous teacher of science (at MIT). For these productions Ambrosino reassembled some of the *NOVA* and *Odyssey* production people. "[My production friends] are a very important part of my life. We keep in touch, have reunions, critique each other's proposals . . . it's an extended family of gifted men and women—and now lots of kids!"

His last production found him back on camera after twenty years: a ninety-minute special produced with Gillian Barnes, "Journey to the Occupied Lands," for WGBH's *Frontline* series. The controversial program, revealing life under occupation in the West Bank and Gaza, was, he says, "an unforgettable experience; a long research period, difficult filming, endless editing, a very favorable response to the broadcast, and . . . organized attacks from the far-right Israeli supporters in the U.S."

Ambrosino, now sixty-seven, is closing his production company and, after forty-two years in public television, trying to design a new life without TV and film and Lillian, who occupied an office next to his for four decades. He has been helping build a post-and-beam barn in Vermont, walking in the Tetons, sailing in the Virgin Islands, white-water rafting and kayaking, attending open rehearsals of the Boston Symphony, taking courses in music theory, and, as always, doing a lot of reading.

Michael Ambrosino is one of a growing number of persons whose professional lives have been spent almost entirely within public television, people whose careers began soon after the first channels were assigned for noncommercial use in 1952. In some sense their talents have advanced in parallel with public television itself. "I am very fortunate that my professional life and the early days of public broadcasting came along together," he says. "There were opportunities to create programs . . . and institutions that had a real staying power. I am delighted that *NOVA* is having its twenty-fifth year and that public broadcasting has become a staple in the intellectual life of Americans."

I recently asked him if he would name some public TV producers he particularly admired. His response: "I admire Fred Rogers' honor, Bill Moyers' sense of mission, Jack Willis' *(The Great American Dream Machine)* sense of news and humor, Russ Morash's *(This Old House)* competency, David Fanning's fairness, Fred Barzyk's *(What's Happening, Mr. Silver?)* daring, Jac Venza's taste, Henry Hampton's guts, Jonathan Rice's *(KQED's Newsroom)* and Judy Crichton's *(The American Experience)* noses for good programs, [and a lot of others] who have put out an astonishing lot of good programs against all odds."

In such company the inventor of *NOVA* would no doubt find a warm welcome.

16

The American Experience

"To clarify an ever-changing present and inform the future with wisdom."

—a wall inscription at Dunbarton Oaks
Byzantine Research Center in Washington D.C.

On a warm summer day in 1946 I find myself, somewhat improbably, at the helm of a U.S. Navy ocean tug, threading through a crowded, palm-fringed Pacific atoll called Bikini. We stay only long enough to anchor the derelict ship we've towed here from the Philippines. Several days later, making slow progress east to Honolulu, we learn that the wreck we had pulled into that pristine island sanctuary had been obliterated—along with everything else in the lagoon—by two atomic bombs. More than a few of my shipmates are bitter that, unlike others, they had been denied an extremely close look at the destruction. But for most of us it is simply an isolated event, one among many in those rather bewildering post-war days following the bombings at Hiroshima and Nagasaki.

Now fast-forward forty-two years to October 1988. I am watching "Radio Bikini," the second program in a new public television history series called *The American Experience*. More than four decades after the bombing, I learn from Robert Stone's film that the Bikini explosions were ordered by the U.S. Navy in order to make a propaganda movie (never completed) at a time when the U.N. was debating strategies for

177

controlling atomic energy. The program explains how inhabitants of the island were uprooted and, even now, are not permitted to return because of high levels of contamination. Nearly forty-two thousand armed forces, politicians, diplomats, and reporters observed as the bombs were dropped over the island. I sit transfixed, watching sailors inspecting the site just *hours* after the detonations, then setting Geiger counters buzzing when they return to their ships. Many who reported sick were told they were probably suffering from food poisoning. They left for home to begin dying slow deaths.

Admiral William Blandy supervised the operation. He and Admiral F. J. Lowery and their wives posed for photographs, beaming at a celebratory cake in the shape of a mushroom cloud. Mrs. Blandy wore a fancy hat adorned with a similar cloud-like puff. I think of my ship companions who felt betrayed when they missed all this.

Fast-forward again: it is now a June day in 1998, more than fifty years since the U.S. demonstration of power in the Pacific. India and Pakistan have set off "tests" of nuclear weapons. "The nuclear club" has become a familiar, largely innocuous phrase. Bikini is a style of swim suit. George Santayana's well-worn phrase ("Those who cannot remember the past are condemned to repeat it") has finally taken up permanent residence in my consciousness. "Radio Bikini," the second chapter in an increasingly complex TV history called *The American Experience*, has clarified a critically important dimension of our present life, and perhaps its future.

When *The American Experience* series began its broadcasting life on October 11, 1988, those associated with its creation held high hopes that it would be a long one; not just that the series would continue to be produced, but that its programs would have more staying power and effectiveness than most TV material. Judy Crichton, executive producer from the beginning until her retirement in 1997, recently reflected upon this: "Very early on I was struck by the fact that those who work in television were turning out a disposable product. By the time I got to WGBH, I didn't want to do that anymore. I wanted to make films that had an ongoing life. I think that if I'm proud of one thing that would be it."

During her years with WGBH, Boston, the series turned out one hundred films. However enduring their substance, their longevity has unquestionably been improved by brisk video sales to schools and the general public (the total is now approaching 275,000) and their influence extended by a web site that now occupies a full-time staff member. A no-nonsense professional with a sternly pragmatic approach to TV production, Crichton is clearly moved when she describes conversations with teachers using *The American Experience* programs in their classrooms.

Peter McGhee, for many years the Boston station's vice president for national programs, calls the series a "place-holder for the intent to make history come alive on public television."

"It will undergo nuanced changes," he says, "as executive producers change. But essentially it has infinite capacity . . . to make sense of our history, and find stories that illuminate both the past and the present."

The American Experience owes much to the thirteen-hour series *Vietnam, A Television History* that McGhee began planning in the late 1970s. *Vietnam* became a major event in public television's program history when it was aired in 1985. The series was brought back by *The American Experience* in the 1996–97 season. "Television was the means by which a generation was educated about Vietnam," says McGhee. "We decided there was a lot [more] American history that fell into that category."

Plans for some sort of American history series began to take shape in 1985 when McGhee asked Marilyn Mellowes, one of his staff members, to prepare a background paper and a proposal for funds to study the prospects for producing an extended American history anthology. It was sent to the National Endowment for the Humanities. A copy went to Ron Hull, then director of the CPB Television Program Fund. The humanities endowment turned it down, but Hull was enthusiastic.

"Ron liked the idea of history," says McGhee, "but thought it should be about the American *experience*. I think he had in mind something much more contemporary—like how it felt to be an American. But Ron's expression found resonance in the title.

"We assembled a group of station managers, created a large editorial board, and did a fair amount of consulting on the way to the SPC," says

McGhee. (The SPC was the Station Program Cooperative, the stations' major means of voting financial support for PBS programs.)

In the summer of 1986 WGBH hosted a two-day seminar in Cambridge, Massachusetts, inviting TV and film producers, public TV executives, and historians. Here there were many expressions concerning the importance of history by nationally recognized scholars, including David Kennedy, professor of history at Stanford. He, and others drawn from Harvard, Boston University, Yale, MIT, and the University of Wisconsin, became the project's first advisory board.

Not unexpectedly, the Cambridge conference produced a large number of lofty aspirations: the series would "use the past to challenge the assumptions of the present and thereby assist in the process of reflection and rejuvenation that is the mark of a vital culture." There was also a certain amount of debunking history as it had been taught in the past, resulting in popular disdain for names and dates because there had been no "narrative to give them drama." Henry Ford was evoked, a man who said that history was "bunk" (and later spent much of his fortune constructing a museum of American life).

The specific design of a series was not neglected: it would "bring together reliable scholarship with experienced and aspiring filmmakers"; it would be "primarily a series of documentary films"; "it will have to show that history is as complex as the present, and just as lively."

According to McGhee, one of the first bridges to be crossed was the chronological approach to history. "The historians we talked to—the best in American history," he says, "rebelled against the notion that there was a history that could be reduced to some chronological account. What we came to understand was that there were many histories of people and groups of people. History presented chronologically was a very old fashioned and discredited idea, one that, not surprisingly, TV critics held to firmly—a set of accepted events along a chain of time."

If *The American Experience* was not history in the sense that TV critics, and perhaps others, were prepared to accept, what was it? Those who planned the new programs had an answer, of sorts: "It will do for history what *NOVA* has done for science." WGBH's *NOVA* had been on the air since 1973 and in this time had become firmly established as television's premier science anthology, each week treating a different subject.

The linkage worked. TV critics who had agonized over explanations of *NOVA* when it first appeared (some publishers commissioning essays on science rather than attempting descriptions of the early programs) now repeated the WGBH mantra: "It will do for history what *NOVA* did for science."

"Basically," continues McGhee, "we were trying to sell PBS and CPB on the priority that should be given to this subject . . . . I think it's fair to say that we were successful. We hired Judy [Crichton] when we had the certainty of one [fully financed] season. She made the second and third SPC presentations. We got three seasons financed before there was a program on the air." (Those who have observed producers presenting program concepts to a gathering of more than two hundred skeptical, independently minded station representatives will recognize this as a considerable achievement.)

Judy Crichton had come prepared. Forty-two years earlier she had helped her father, Ben Feiner, provide CBS television coverage of the 1944 elections. He had one camera, a secretary, and his daughter, who kept voter tallies on a blackboard. Earlier, Feiner had worked as a radio reporter for WKNY ("The voice of the Hudson Valley") with Judy as his "spotter" at sports events and parades.

"He was a great reader," she remembers, "especially of popular historical works." Her own formal education was sketchy. She left high school when she was sixteen (but not before delivering the class paper: "Wither Video?"). "Fortunately," she says, "I married a brilliant man [Robert Crichton] when I was fairly young. He said, 'First, you'll have to read *War and Peace* and lose twenty pounds.' *War and Peace* was easier."

After a few years as a researcher for *This Week* magazine, she joined the (now defunct) Dumont Television Network in 1949. "In those days," she says, "everyone in TV did everything. I was the secretary, the researcher, did the [audience] warm-ups, hawked tickets at Rockefeller Center, tried to explain the image orthicon camera to tourists, and wrote questions for quizzes. I had four kids and a husband who was trying to be a novelist so I didn't do much traveling. I had never spent a night in a hotel until I was in my late thirties.

"By 1973 I had put on lots of TV shows, although I was an associate producer—for seventeen years. In those days no woman was given the title of producer."

One day she ran across Bill Leonard, then president of CBS News, and asked him for a job. "I was the first woman producer at *CBS Reports* and did many shows there that I'm still proud of: 'The CIA's Secret Army,' 'The Battle for South Africa,' two programs in a five-part series entitled *The Defense of the United States,* among others."

There were several job offers from WGBH during this time but she turned them down. "My husband was ill, my kids were college age. I needed the security that CBS could provide. In 1981 I went to ABC where I was very happy until they disbanded their documentary unit."

McGhee and Crichton had been friends for many years, having met on Martha's Vineyard where both spent some part of their summers.

"He [McGhee] called and asked if I wanted to do this [history series]. He said in no uncertain terms that I was getting a bit long in the tooth, and implied that if I were going to jump I had better do it then or not be invited again."

"At the time we asked Judy to become executive producer," says McGhee, "she was beginning to run on empty as far as commercial television is concerned. Her first assignment was to build a staff and develop programs." Throughout her supervision of *The American Experience* she continued to live in New York, spending three days a week in Boston.

"I chose the first program of the series ['The San Francisco Earthquake of 1906'] for three reasons," she says. "First, because it is a helluva story. Second, it was nearing a time when witnesses to the event were few and becoming fewer. And third, I wanted to prove to myself—and everybody else—that you could build tension and excitement using still photographs and a really good, strong script.

"By that time Ken Burns had produced 'The Brooklyn Bridge,' but it was a short film, not an hour. It was very good but it used a lot of modern film. I wanted films that got back in time and *stayed* there—visually as well as in terms of the narrative."

The New York Times' John O'Connor welcomed *The American Experience* by calling it "an umbrella series, encompassing a variety of documentaries within the confines of a sketchy theme," noting that it would be produced by "first-class professionals."

Time recognized the first show by placing it on the magazine's "Critics' Choice" list along with Liberace. John Carmen of the *San Francisco Chronicle* described "The San Francisco Earthquake" as "a fiery film history that sizzles and crackles and pulls together heaps of data and interviews with survivors into a cohesive and dramatically told story." Crichton, who had been very unhappy at ABC before her departure, must have been pleased at a comparison in the *Boston Globe's* review: "The ABC program [*Our World*] left you with the impression that the producers and writers began with the film footage and built their stories around it, whereas the PBS show seems to begin with the story then looks for the best way to illustrate it."

Before the series commenced, reviewers were sent information on all programs in the first season. The subjects were nothing if not varied, a smorgasbord as had been intended, drawn from a wide spectrum of American history: a Mississippi exploration in 1832, the lives of factory women in World War II, the evolution of rhythm and blues, Geronimo's Apache resistance in 1886, profiles of Eudora Welty and Robert Moses.

Some reviewers seemed perplexed. Some called the series eclectic, and others, as McGhee had foreseen, complained about the lack of continuity, the chronological linkages they had found in earlier productions such as *Alistair Cooke's America*.

CPB, thanks largely to Ron Hull's persuasive advocacy, was a prominent funder of the first season. The corporation, once criticized for supporting bold documentaries, now found itself taken to task (by the *Boston Herald*) for "no longer giving full support to controversial works." Some objected to the series' title: "Saying nothing and saying something at the same time," remarked Thomas Fleming, author and historian. "A collection, perhaps, but not a series."

Meanwhile, Crichton and her senior producer, Margaret Drain (whom Crichton had hired from CBS to join the original staff) continued to commission and acquire films with a professionalism born of talent and long experience. "It was not that different from what we'd done in the past," Crichton remembers. "It was some time before the good reviews came in. But it was one of those things where we had so much *enthusiasm*. I seldom say this about projects I work on because by nature I'm always running scared. But *American Experience* was such a damn good idea! It just seemed so logical that it gave us all spine."

One of the most encouraging early press reactions was not in a TV column but an editorial in the Canby (Oregon) *Herald* (circulation 4,310): "It may seem strange for a newspaper to urge people to watch a television program, but *The American Experience* . . . deserves recognition and promotion."

It was clear before the series began that universal acceptance by audiences, critics, and public TV executives would not come easily. "There were enormous misgivings and misunderstandings," says Crichton. "When you said history to people in those days, there was a tacit assumption that you were going to present a chronology, and were therefore going to start in the seventeenth century with the colonists and march through time. No one could imagine pulling in an audience for that. The public TV stations saw it as potentially *very* boring."

The series needed a host, someone who could supply historical credibility and the continuity that many felt was absent. "David was my idea," says Crichton. David McCullough was a historian and author whose work included books on the Panama Canal, the Brooklyn Bridge, Theodore Roosevelt, and the Johnstown flood. Moreover, he had TV experience as host for *Smithsonian World*, a distinguished series produced by the federal museum agency. Like McGhee and Crichton, McCullough spent his summers on Martha's Vineyard. Crichton, although familiar with his books, had never seen him in person—until he began to speak at a town meeting on the island, discussing a road maintenance problem.

"When he stood up and spoke he was so brilliant and easy that I thought, 'My God, he is absolutely perfect as the host.'"

In addition to his on-air duties for *The American Experience*, McCullough has contributed much by way of his frequent statements of support for the series. McGhee notes that Crichton introduced McCullough to station executives when she went before them to ask for second-season financing. A man who has rarely misjudged the stations' attachment to conservative, tested talent, McGhee says, soberly, "He gave them reassurance."

In a widely distributed Associated Press interview with Kathryn Baker in the early days of the series, McCullough explains that he became involved in history through looking at photographs of the subject he eventually described in writing. "When imaginative and talented people start nosing around in old films and [photographs]," he says, "they're going to... reveal aspects of our nature that we haven't even thought about." He is frequently quoted on the inadequacies of teaching history in the classroom, the power of well-told stories, and the effective historian's interest in people: "It is my experience that if you simply tell what has happened, it is so fascinating, so human, you don't have to sugar-coat the pill, you don't have to devise a means to pull people into the subject. They'll come in because there's nothing more interesting than what has happened to people. And that's all history is."

Among the papers flowing from the conference that defined the hopes for *The American Experience*, there was considerable emphasis upon the interaction between scholars and filmmakers: "An active and lively partnership" was one description. In 1996 David Grubin, producer of several presidential documentaries for the series—"LBJ," "Theodore Roosevelt," and "Truman"—reported some of his encounters with scholarly committees: "[They] review the script and the film at several points during its development." In the process of his Theodore Roosevelt biography he argued with historians about whether or not T.R. was "attracted to war" and whether or not he had an "almost messianic" belief in his own destiny. (They also discussed whether a flag was at "half-mast" or "half-staff.") "The biggest difficulty with historical advis-ers," says Grubin, "is that they want to see more than you can ever do."

Crichton acknowledges that initially the historians viewed the TV producers with considerable suspicion, perhaps with good reason: "There weren't many producers then who had worked in the field of his-tory, and very few who had used still photographs. The historians were not used to translating printed material to film. Film is a very chintzy medium. If you pack too much information into a film, people can't hear it, can't absorb it. And so for all of us—historians, producers, writ-ers—there was a real period of learning. We were trying to design film economically, to carry the maximum amount of information and yet not destroy the power of the narrative or overwhelm the viewer."

Margaret Drain, senior producer of the series since its beginning, became its second executive producer in January 1997. Like her predecessor she is the daughter of a TV producer. When she was a child, both of her par-ents worked for pioneering station WLW in Cincinnati. Following parochial school she graduated from Marquette University (English and history), taught English as a second language in Boston, and spent a year as an *au pair* in France. In 1976 she graduated from the Columbia School of Journalism where she met Fred Friendly, the venerated, influential CBS producer with whom she later worked in the communications division of the Ford Foundation. She produced programs at New York's WNET (*Bill Moyers' Journal*) for two years before moving to CBS News. There she pro-duced programs with Charles Kuralt and for *CBS Reports*. It was at CBS that she met Judy Crichton, who later invited her to WGBH.

These days Drain and her staff receive about three hundred produc-tion proposals each year (down from nearly four hundred earlier). They come in various stages of development—from concepts to partial pro-ductions, but few completed films (an exception was "Ridin' the Rails," about teenaged hoboes in the '30s). There are fewer acquisitions now than in the past. Nearly half of the programs were purchased in the first season. The total budget is now about $9 million, an increase of nearly $2 million since 1988.

From start to finish, completion of an average production requires between eight and nine months. "We try to give people as much research time as possible," says Drain. "Producers work on the narrative for four or five weeks or longer. We are critically interested in where the story is going and spend a lot of time on that. The producer must have a sense of how much archival material is available and how to fill out the story if it isn't. Producers check in periodically, some more than others. Some productions are extremely complex."

The series has been known for giving producers sufficient time to do their homework. "There are two kinds of time," says Crichton, "one that is enormously expensive—once the editing doors open. If you try to shake out your thinking at that juncture, you nearly always get into budget trouble. We sometimes said to people, 'You're not prepared yet to go out and shoot' or 'You're not prepared to open the editing room.' We'd demand an awful lot of paperwork before we let people get going."

Drain and Crichton agree that writing is the most important element in *American Experience* documentaries. Crichton puts it this way: "Good writing is essential. If you don't do it with imagination, energy, and grace, [the program] is just a confection."

David McCullough, who writes his own material to introduce the programs (usually preparing and recording descriptions for two or three programs in a day), has often commented upon the programs' stories: "We tell stories, authentic American stories for their own great fascination, the pull of narrative, and often because they are so particularly revealing about who we are and how we got to where we are. One of the aspects of a good story is getting the hero down a well and then up again. One of the most interesting ways to learn about history is to see how character manifests itself during crisis."

Drain and Crichton say that some of the most frustrating productions were ultimately the most satisfying, especially programs that lacked archival material and needed to rely upon a strong script— "The Way West" and "The Donner Party," for example. Of the latter program Crichton says that it is "put together by spit and mirrors, Ric Burns and Lisa Ades' genius, and a very strong narrative. You could give a filmmaking class by turning off the sound on 'The Donner Party' and you'd think nothing has happened."

The audience for *The American Experience* remains remarkably unchanged in total number (about seven million) as well as composition (predominately male, 31 percent with college degrees and family incomes over sixty thousand dollars). Disaster films ("The Johnstown Flood," "Influenza 1918," "The San Francisco Earthquake") remain the most popular along with programs on flying ("Lindbergh," "Amelia Earhart," and "The Wright Stuff"). (Not surprisingly, these are the topics *NOVA* audiences likewise find most attractive.)

As the series has matured, multiple programs on one subject have taken on larger significance. Many of these have been presidential portraits. "When we aired the two-part 'Nixon' in the third season," says Drain, "we knew we were on to something." Seven presidential biographies have followed—"LBJ," "The Kennedys," "Ike," "FDR," "T.R.," "Truman," and "Reagan." In addition to their gratifying broadcast ratings (the five-part "The Kennedys" was the most popular PBS mini-series since Ken Burns' *The Civil War*), they have enjoyed lively video sales and, by 1998, millions of "hits" on the series' web site.

"What we began to do with those films," says Crichton, "was to structure them . . . like novels, so that you have a sense of where the characters are when they're off-screen. 'The Kennedys' had a big cast of characters. It began to happen in that film. There's a very novelistic quality to the films on LBJ and Theodore Roosevelt. I had always wanted to do a documentary version of *The Jewel in the Crown,* and I felt working on those films—'Nixon' and 'The Kennedys'—that we were beginning to approach that kind of work, where the story had a really strong narrative drive and the filming and editing were up to the script. You came out of it with a richness that was rare."

Those associated with the presidential productions, indeed the entire output of *The American Experience,* seem keenly aware of how time and contemporary perceptions can modify events. "We'll always have a president in our sights," says Peter McGhee, "whether Grant or Jimmy Carter or whoever. But it's very important that you let the dust settle a bit so that you can begin to make the first rough estimate. We couldn't have made the Vietnam series in 1973, when the helicopters were taking off the roof in Saigon. I think if someone looked at the [Vietnam] experience now, it would look a lot differently than it looked to us."

"I think part of the success of *The American Experience*," says Crichton, "was that I never felt any of these films was definitive, that one could always go back and tell what you didn't have time to deal with originally." Crichton says she tried to plan several documentaries of the same event ("a real *Rashomon*"). "You would need hugely talented people," she says. "It was often under consideration but we never pulled it off."

"The Kennedys," a coproduction with Britain's Thames Television, required two years to complete. David Espar, one of the producers, has said that while there was an enormous amount of material, the best narrative thread was difficult to find. "It was the kind of thing you can only do as a filmmaker if you have plenty of time. You sit there with these images and sounds for quite a while, figuring out how you're going to put the pieces together to make the connections and tell the story," citing the moment when JFK doffs his hat to his father at his inauguration: "It distilled that moment for which the elder Kennedy had labored so long."

Here is Adrianna Bosche who, with Austin Hoyt, produced "Reagan": "We had to cut through his optimism and rosy recollections to discover a nomadic childhood, an alcoholic father, a religious mother, and the defining moment of his youth—summers spent as a lifeguard on the Rock River, where he rescued seventy-seven people. That role as rescuer combined with his youthful optimism played itself out on ever larger stages as Reagan defined his political agenda."

Hoyt, a veteran WGBH producer, reflects that "it takes time for themes and a story to emerge. All the while you have to be open to new traits, unexpected turns, that send you back to reconstruct what you thought you knew, so that in the end you get the story right."

"Producers need to have a kind of generosity," says Crichton, "that allows them to move past their own assumptions. It's absurd to think that anyone old enough to produce a film doesn't have an opinion. But the responsibility is to accept the fact that you have an opinion, and that it might be wrong, you might be misinformed, you may not know enough."

As *The American Experience* rolls into its second decade, virtually all criticism that it didn't present history chronologically has long vanished—it disappeared largely after the second season. The series' historians and program producers continue to tell disparate stories. And many of the stories seem to ask, implicitly, "Why bother? Why do we care, why should we care, about history?" Toward the end of a *Current* interview with Judy Crichton in 1997, she gives an answer: "All the boring things that everybody tells you are absolutely true, which is there is no way you can know yourself if you don't know where you come from. That is true both of your psyche and your cultural and political background.... You can say you don't like your own background. You can shift, you can change, you can reject it, you can do anything you want with it, but in order to make any of those decisions...you have to know where you came from and where your folks came from."

Few would disagree that history is, certainly can be, immensely compelling. David McCullough supplies an explanation for this in his introduction to the series' fifth season: "It is the very unexpectedness that draws us in. What happened...and then, of course, what happened next, and why? Our need to know is as real as gravity. But then life is about change. So perhaps we have the essence of it; the pull of history is life."

Or as a friend of mine once said to me—ironically, because it was shortly before his untimely and unexpected death—"The thing I'll dislike most about dying is not knowing how things turned out."

17

Frontline

"The only regularly scheduled long-form public affairs series on American television." That's what its producers say about *Frontline*, and although numberless TV services continue to emerge like weeds in an untended garden, I have found no reason to dispute this description. By January 1998, as *Frontline* embarked upon its sixteenth season, its relentlessly adversarial programs had conspired to offend nearly every sector of contemporary society. It has been rewarded for this highly democratic achievement by consistently large audiences as well as more than fifty major broadcasting honors, including twenty-five Emmys and four Peabodys. Two Alfred I. duPont "golden batons" have been bestowed upon it for "contributions to the world of exceptional journalism."

Peter McGhee, Vice President of WGBH/Boston where *Frontline* is created, explains that he found its executive producer, David Fanning, "on a beach in California," a story not altogether at odds with Fanning's own account of how he was recruited in 1977—first to produce *World, Frontline*'s predecessor.

Prior to his lengthy WGBH engagement, Fanning lived a somewhat nomadic life. Here he talks to Michael Ambrosino in 1997; he is describing his childhood in a middle-class suburb of Port Elizabeth, South Africa: "My mother read books and my father built boats. A great stream of books came from the library every day. They were always around. By the time I was a teenager I was reading a lot of biographies, autobiographies, and some great travel books.

"My father traveled and adventured and read constantly—books about people who would sail off around the world. He ran an Outward Bound school. My mother went to the university and did history and classics. My father was pulled out of the schoolyard and trained as a carpenter and joiner—a cabinet maker. He didn't want me to work with my hands. He wanted a life of the mind for me."

David Edward Fanning, one of public television's leading executive producers for nearly twenty years, was born in 1951. His father's hobby was building wooden boats, twelve to twenty feet long, in a shed at the bottom of the family's garden. He constructed nearly seventy of them during his lifetime. "He did it by instinct," says his son. "He'd loft the curve of a boat by sight and would draw a a waterline on it before it ever floated. I have a great appreciation for the making of things. He was a man for whom the joint at the back of the cabinet was as important as the one you could see; at the same time a carpenter willing to use any tool, no matter how crude, to get the job done. I think there was something in the making of boats . . . the joinery . . . the fitting together of two pieces . . . that is at the heart of what I love. And from my mother [I received] a love of words."

His father and mother had been born in England where one of his grandmothers had been an actress. They were brought to South Africa separately when they were children. "I always felt we were visitors," Fanning says. "This dusty place that was inhabited by other people. We had a little house on a river . . . sand dunes and a lagoon, and monkeys in the trees. I still go looking for that sense of solitude in a place."

These days, the middle-aged executive producer of *Frontline*, who has been variously described as "slightly eccentric," "an elite cultural authority," and "a cross between a gypsy and a college professor," lives in Marblehead, just north of Boston, a place from which he commutes driving a Toyota pick-up truck. He windsurfs and sometimes goes fishing in a small boat. Recently he has spent a month each year studying painting in Italy.

By the time WGBH invited him to come to Boston to supervise the production of a new series, *World*, Fanning had completed his formal education and had produced documentaries in South Africa, England, and the U.S. After twelve years of school in Port Elizabeth, he commenced Naval training. This was interrupted when he received a scholarship to study for a year in a California high school. Returning to South Africa, he completed his national service and entered the University of Cape Town, again on a scholarship, to study marine biology. Here he discovered that, while he could do the work, science was not where he belonged. "So I bailed," he says. "I offered to give up the scholarship and pay it off." The Anglo-American Foundation told him it wasn't necessary and wished him luck.

During his first college year he worked for the *Eastern Province Herald,* reporting brush fires and the shipping news. Later he went to Johannesburg and became a writer for a weekly magazine. Here a feature story about a director who had produced a movie concerning an interracial love affair led to his first film experience. He became an assistant on a low-budget movie shot in a small town—a brief episode he now describes as hilarious and awful. "The director [about whom he had written] was having an affair with the leading lady who was engaged to the cameraman, while I was learning to load [film] magazines." In the end he was fired when it became known that he had assumed some of the responsibilities of the unit's alcoholic editor. The director told him he was lazy, adding, "I don't think you have a chance of making it in this business anyway."

Suddenly enthralled by filmmaking, he soon borrowed equipment and raised enough money to produce a short documentary called *The Churches of Africa.* This led to a second that concerned the Church and apartheid. He was advised to screen the second film for the BBC. "So," he says, "I sold my motorbike and bought a ticket and went to London with my film under my arm." *The Church and Apartheid* was his first film for broadcast. He might have remained at the BBC but, as he says, "It was too closed. I was going to have to surmount the Oxbridge and colonial barriers [and] I was a bit intimidated, I think." He recalls standing in the BBC Club on a drizzly October evening with the smell of damp wool and stale beer and, amidst the loud voices, saying, "I think I'll go to California." Which he did by the end of the week.

He returned to Newport Beach, to the family with whom he had lived when on his earlier scholarship. Here he learned that a new public TV station, KOCE, was opening in Huntington Beach on the campus of Golden State College, and he soon met Don Gerdts, the head of programming. "They never got rid of me," he says. "I was there volunteering and being around, and suddenly somebody got another job and I became a cinematographer-editor." Fanning describes the next four years (1973–77) as one of his "great gigs." "We had a refrigerator full of film we had to shoot for the weekly series and a film van we could use. We each had a Steenbeck in our office, and we made things." One of the documentaries he made looked ahead to the twentieth anniversary of the *Brown versus the Board of Education* Supreme Court decision—*Deep South, Deep North,* a coproduction with the BBC. This was an unusual venture for KOCE and an important step in Fanning's career.

He then made a film entitled *The Agony of Independence,* about the Angolan civil war, and sent it to PBS, where it was distributed nationally. The production budget was just under fifteen thousand dollars.

Anxious to repeat this experience, he wrote several proposals and forwarded them to PBS. One concerned "international hot spots." All of them languished at the network for months. PBS seemed "interested but uncertain." Eventually, Peter McGhee who had seen the proposals, phoned from WGBH. "Do you have any plans to visit Boston?" he enquired. "No," Fanning replied. McGhee then said he would soon be in California and could see him on his way to San Francisco. They met at the Los Angeles airport. Fanning drove McGhee to Newport Beach, all the while answering questions about his work for KOCE. McGhee then gave him a proposal to read. It described a series of twelve one-hour programs, eventually entitled *World.* There followed a period of indecision during which Fanning weighed the idea of becoming an executive producer, even going to Boston to talk seriously about the job. Others, he soon learned, were quite interested in the position. At length, following a protracted period of interviews and discussions, he was offered, and accepted, the job.

During his four years at KOCE he had produced a dozen films. By

January 1998 he had turned out nearly four hundred public affairs documentaries, first for *World* then for *Frontline*.

In Boston in 1977 he set about assembling a staff for *World*. Some of the producers would eventually work for *Frontline*: they included Bill Cran, a producer for Canada's CBC; Ofra Bikel, who had made programs for WNET and Israeli TV; David Kuhn; and Judy Vecchione. The purpose of *World* was to bring international documentaries to an American audience. According to Fanning, the programs were to resemble pieces in *The New Yorker*, "surprising and unexpected." There are frequent references to *The New Yorker*, especially its literate and literary characteristics, in Fanning's descriptions of his work. Like its quirky, immensely talented former editor, William Shawn, Fanning sees himself dispatching reporters into the world, who return to tell him what they have found. Editors, he believes, should add a sense of wonder. Reflecting upon stories and literary style (something he does often), he says, "I think that's at the heart of who we are as human beings. We still sit around the fire and look for someone to tell us stories of great journeys." A good story-teller himself, Fanning looks just for stories, then for "topics." "We talk up to our audience," he has said, "and assume they're prepared to settle into serious subjects . . . on the condition that we tell a crackling good story."

One of the first was commissioned from an accomplished story-teller, Ved Mehta, whose stories Fanning had read as a university student and, perhaps not coincidentally, a writer for *The New Yorker*. He sent Mehta, who is blind, to his homeland, India, with producer Bill Cran, thinking, "a film by a blind man would be interesting." Mehta later wrote a book about the experience, *The Photographs of Chachajii*. The subject was one of Mehta's poor relatives, "a survivor on the edge of the abyss of Indian poverty, clinging to his dignity." Fanning reports having made some helpful remarks about the film when it was being edited, comments, he says, Mehta later attributed to himself. Today Fanning recalls the production as "one of the really extraordinary films of *World*. It was made because of editorial gut; you know, instinct. There was a kind of impresario quality

to what I did. I sought out Ved Mehta. I brought these two parties together, made that marriage and said, 'Go. I will trust what you do.' They
went off and discovered that film in the field. But that's, of course, what
Frontline does to this day. I think that William Shawn of *The New Yorker*
did the same thing. It is the literary content. In the details he's both the
rhythms and the aesthetic. It's what raises it from being documentary
news footage to something... larger which has a literary quality. It is
raised to the level of art. It is the accretion of detail [providing] time for
the writer to find it ... and for the reader to absorb it."

Recruiting producers for *World,* Fanning recalls, "We did have the
pick of the bunch at that time. Anything that was out there we could
get. There were no cable channel competitors, and we mixed up a lot of
different styles. It was a chance to say to American documentarians as
well as the audience, 'Hey, there are a lot of ways you can slice this
world... and serve it up.' There were a lot of different voices, and I was
very aware of the hand of the author."

Fanning often speaks of documentaries representing "a truth"; not a
defense, he believes, but an explanation of filmmakers' shooting and editing decisions: "It [television] is the most manipulative of media. And
it is only as honest as its practitioners."

In 1979 Fanning collaborated with Anthony Thomas to make a film
entitled "Death of a Princess." It was in part a docudrama. Shot in Beirut
and Egypt, it concerned the beheading of a Saudi princess who had
been accused and convicted of having a love affair with a man who was
likewise put to death. The program caused an uproar. The Saudi Royal
family protested vehemently. Fanning and Thomas were sued for $20
billion on behalf of seven hundred million Muslims, a suit subsequently
dismissed. The U.S. State Department attempted to intervene (without
success) to have the broadcast canceled, with then Deputy Secretary of
State Warren Christopher taking the lead in this action. The public TV
station in Houston refused to carry the program. Mobil Oil, a major
WGBH contributor, was more than somewhat irked, and when pressure
was applied to PBS, WGBH investigated how to air the program independently on a satellite, something that proved unnecessary. To all of

this Fanning responded with remarkable insouciance that the anger which fell upon him "was not sought nor anticipated."

Following "Death of a Princess," broadcast in May 1980, Fanning took a leave of absence from WGBH and went to Hollywood to begin writing a screenplay. Here he became intrigued with the production of another documentary—once again created with Anthony Thomas—"Confessions of a Dangerous Man." The subject, Frank Terpel, was a renegade ex-CIA agent turned gun-runner who was attempting to evade Libyan and Syrian intelligence as well as the wife he had neglected to divorce before marrying another woman. Terpel's escapades took Fanning to Damascus, Beirut, and elsewhere. "Confessions..." was to become one of the last programs for *World.*

Seeking funding to complete the Terpel film, Fanning went to Washington to meet Lewis Freedman, director of the recently created Program Fund of the Corporation for Public Broadcasting (CPB). The two men had much in common, not least their love of literature. Fanning's program aspirations—"We see ourselves publishing major literate works in television"—would have appealed to Freedman. The range of Freedman's reading was exceptionally broad, frequently reaching into esoterica. To make a point during a conversation with him, I once cited a favorite story by Thomas Mann, one I had first read as a boy in a volume entitled *Stories of Three Decades.* Freedman nodded, quoted some long passages from the tale, then described, in considerable detail, the rough oatmeal-colored cloth cover of the edition I had mentioned.

Lewis Freedman, who died in 1992 at age sixty-six, was himself an exceptionally gifted producer and program executive, perhaps the most talented program maker in public TV's relatively short history. A 1946 graduate of Harvard, he first went to work as a stage manager for CBS, the network for which he later produced the much-esteemed Sunday morning series *Camera Three,* and later created *Play of the Week* for Channel 13 in New York. His production of *The Andersonville Trial* for public television's *Hollywood Television Theatre* brought him a Peabody award and an Emmy for the best program of 1970. He was a founder and cultural affairs director of the Ford Foundation–financed Public Broadcasting Laboratory, produced the "'Bicentennial Minutes" for CBS, and is said to have developed the concept of *Sesame Street* with his friend, Joan Ganz Cooney, the first president of Children's Television Workshop. While Director of CPB's Program Fund he helped to establish the series *Wonderworks, American Playhouse, Crises to Crises,* and *Matters of Life and Death* as well as *Frontline*.

Freedman took Fanning around the corner for a deli sandwich. When they returned Fanning began to describe *World*. As he remembers the conversation, Freedman listened patiently, finally saying, "'That's all very interesting, but what if it was about the United States, much more about domestic subjects?' And I said, 'Well, that would be interesting: *World* could come home.' And he said, 'What if it was weekly?' And I said, 'Well, yes, weekly, but how many weeks?' He said, 'How about twenty-six weeks?' And I said, 'That's a lot of weeks to do an hour-long series.' He said, 'What do you think it would cost?' And I said, 'Six million dollars.' And he said, 'Well, if I were to put up five million the first year, do you think you could get another million from the stations?' And I said, 'If I made a guarantee of five million the first year, four million the second, and three million the third year, do you think the stations would make a three-year commitment?' And I said, 'Yes' without having any idea that they would, at the same time utterly terrified by what he was saying and not even suggesting that I should do the series."

In fact Freedman did ask eventually, "Is this something you want to do?" Fanning said he was unsure. It would remove him from hands-on production. He was enjoying his present work and dabbling in screenplays. He knew others who could, and probably would, do it. But in the end he agreed to become *Frontline's* executive producer.

Freedman insisted that, while the series would be based at WGBH, it should be managed by a consortium of public TV stations (Boston, New York, Miami, Seattle, and Detroit), the same structure that he had put in place for the production of *American Playhouse*. Fanning says he believes the consortium was "effectively a political decision to deal with the warring interests of the bigger stations." Freedman also felt that *Frontline* should not be an anthology, that it should be a work of journalism with the executive producer acting as editor-in-chief; not having editorial "control," as Fanning puts it, so much as editorial "responsibility." This suited Fanning and was later staunchly supported by Freedman when the series came under considerable pressure from independent producers, many of whom felt disadvantaged by this arrangement.

A governing board representing members of the consortium was established as well as an editorial advisory committee to oversee more detailed production matters. Among the advisors not representing public broadcasting interests were Ellen Goodman, a syndicated columnist; Richard Salant, a former president of CBS News; and Lawrence Pinkham, a University of Massachusetts journalism professor. All of this, "the driving force of it," says Fanning, "was Lewis Freedman's decision, a grand gesture."

"I'm not big on writing long proposals," Fanning says. "The one for *Frontline* was based upon *World*. We shot an eight-to-ten minute presentation tape in the GBH control room and cut the footage around it. Then we went into one of those video-around-the-system TV conferences with Larry Grossman and David Ives [presidents, respectively, of PBS and WGBH]. It was a closed-circuit feed to the stations. I answered questions and did the sales job. I made all the promises of what I thought this series could be: investigative, journeys, national politics, and human stories . . ."

There was less than a year to prepare the first programs, and Fanning was worried about finding experienced producers. Mike Kirk was recruited from Seattle and became senior editor. Some of the people were gathered from *World*—Lou Wiley, Judy Vecchione, and Bill Cran. Cran produced *Frontline*'s first program, "An Unauthorized History of the NFL" (a coproduction "poor Bill Cran carried on his back," says Fanning). "Bill is basically cautious but in control. I was enormously respectful of what Bill did [in the Ved Mehta production] and the fact that he would, in turn, listen to me at all.

"We had to jump-start the series and began assigning stories as fast

as we could. At the same time I was confronting the serious and controversial question of the host or anchor . . ." There were a lot of candidates. One, a very well-known tall and imposing correspondent, was
flown in for an interview. He said he was prepared to leave his network
and, when told there were to be twenty-six programs in the series, announced that he would need to be in at least fourteen of them as correspondent. "So," says Fanning, "he got back on the shuttle, because
one thing I didn't want was for somebody to make it his or her own
platform." Dan Shorr, with whom Fanning had worked during the
early days of *World* (and is presently chief correspondent for National
Public Radio), was a strong, if somewhat politically controversial,
prospect. In any event, the question of host and a series' title needed to
be discussed by the advisors.

"Committees are strange beasts," says Fanning. "And unless you
know clearly what you want committees will kill a good idea in a moment because it takes just one nay-sayer for an idea to perish and nobody to rise in its support." Some of the titles in contention were
"Focus," "Focal Point," "National Debate," "First Edition," "Panorama,"
"Spotlight," "On Assignment," and "Close to Home." Planning was
reaching a critical stage. "Frontline," a title Fanning had thought of in
the shower, was finally chosen and funding was committed for two
years by CPB and the public television stations.

But the host/anchor indecision persisted. Then someone mentioned
Jessica Savitch's name "out of the blue." Everyone seemed to have the
impression of a forceful and attractive woman. But few, least of all Fanning, knew much about her. "Essentially," he says, "before we knew
what had happened, Jessica Savitch had signed up . . . and in a way we
were caught a little off-guard, a little naive and, in retrospect, without
enough forethought. To her credit she was a better journalist than most
people thought. She didn't let a script go by that she didn't question.
She wanted to be clear about what she said. And we threw her into the
breach [of the first program]. Bill Cran handled her in the field on that
film and we discovered that she was very troubled and hard to work
with, very insecure; [she] would do her best but sometimes had diffi-

culty sorting out her own insecurity from the job that needed to get done. And we had some second thoughts about what I had got us into. Of course I took a lot of heat around it."

Some members of the advisory group were disapproving. But Jessica Savitch was in place, and there she would remain, for better and worse, throughout the first season. "If anybody had the ability to look into a camera," says Fanning, "and say, 'America, pay attention,' Jessica could do that. We didn't realize how much her star was in danger of disintegrating." By the end of the first year Fanning had made the decision not to renew her contract and went to New York to tell her this. She had been reclusive for some weeks. They met at a restaurant and, although she seemed fragile, she told him she had recently met someone, was beginning a new and important relationship, and seemed happy. "I couldn't break the news to her," he says. "I chickened out. I realized that I would have to write her a letter." This was on a Friday. Early the next Monday morning, Bob Ferrante, a WGBH producer, phoned him to say she was dead. She had drowned in a car that was backed into a canal near a restaurant where she had been having dinner with her new friend.

In 1982 when she joined *Frontline*, Savitch was well known to American TV audiences. She was anchoring NBC's *Nightly News* on Saturday and had written a well-publicized autobiography. *Frontline*'s first press releases announced that she would take "a partial leave of absence" from the network. Says Fanning, "She gave us a kind of presence. People ten years later would say, '*Frontline*? Isn't that the series Jessica Savitch was on?'" On January 13, 1983, she introduced and reported *Frontline*'s first program.

I recall watching "An Unauthorized History of the NFL" when the series premiered, thinking it was an accomplished piece of investigative journalism. It seemed less a product of public TV than a program turned out by a high-budget commercial television network with "production values" that many in public TV then sought; "real television," a little glossy but highly professional and authoritative. Sixteen years later it continues to seem well, perhaps too well, crafted, as if the producers were anxious not to make a misstep by omitting some aspect of documentation or neglecting an important production technique.

Knowing, now, something about the vulnerabilities Jessica Savitch brought to the production, it is difficult not to interpret her intensity as a mask for uncertainty as she speaks to us, clipboard in hand, about gambling's high stakes in professional football. She questions the NFL's commissioner, Pete Rozelle, whose moon-faced boyish expression of innocence remains comically unvaried throughout the interviews. These question periods, conducted in her soft, determined voice, resemble a mother superior unsuccessfully interrogating a wayward nun. More tentative is her one uncertain appearance in a stadium where she must deliver her lines while walking across the screen in a fashionable trench coat. Here she keeps looking down as if she might step on some undesirable object in the grass.

Continuity is occasionally sacrificed as the crime-related pro-football bases are covered. At one point we find ourselves inexplicably whisked to Fort Lauderdale to witness a bookie being observed by undercover cameras and subsequently arrested. This is followed by a demonstration of how written documents may be instantly destroyed. There is a large element of theatricality here, something that neither Fanning nor his *Frontline* producers have ever forsworn in the interests of a good story.

The balletic tumble of football is skillfully edited into the action of Las Vegas, Mafia murders, and the relatively arcane vocabulary of gambling's "runners, agents, wise guys, and beards." One otherwise pedestrian film sequence of uniformed football players emerging (in extremely slow-motion) onto the field from a lower locker room takes on the appearance of monsters being operatically disgorged from some mythical netherworld. "Witnesses" drawn from "high security prisons" provide testimony of payoffs and bribes. We meet Tony ("the ant") Spilatro, Jimmy ("the weasel") Traviano and others whose names are only funny if they are not pointing guns. Some of them appear—often in unintentionally hilarious disguises—to talk about fixing professional games in which the coach as well as the defensive and offensive captains were paid a total of $800,000 (for four games) "to protect," as one witness puts it, "our investment." "The Weasel," taking a long, relaxed pull on his enormous cigar, describes working with referees in the casual, pragmatic way a diamond cutter might explain how he shapes an average-sized stone. "In them days," he says, "they didn't have this television replay."

Frontline paid a fee for these statements, something not lost on many newspapers reviewing the program. Fanning responded in his characteristic matter-of-fact manner that it was not easy to make rules about such things and that, in this case, no one was paid more than three thousand dollars. There were some remarks in print about "checkbook journalism" but surprisingly they seemed not to tarnish the program or damage the new series.

The program's most dramatic feature concerned Carroll Rosenbloom, an NFL team owner and heavy gambler who had reportedly bet against his own team, the Baltimore Colts, before purchasing the Los Angeles Rams. Victor Weiss, who carried Rosenbloom's money, had been killed and his body stuffed into the trunk of a red Rolls Royce. Later, in April 1979, Rosenbloom drowned near his ocean-front Florida home in what some believed was another mobster murder. *Frontline* reopened the incident—which had been ruled an accident—by discovering and interviewing the single witness, a French-Canadian whose recollection suggested that Rosenbloom may have been pulled under by someone. (He also asserted that two men pulled the victim out of the surf, left the body on the beach, telling the Canadian to leave the scene.)

A documentary describing these unsavory goings-on was bound to attract attention, especially as it was scheduled, not coincidentally, in close proximity to the 1983 Super Bowl, the largest gambling event of every U.S. sporting season. As the music rises under Jessica Savitch's earnestness, she promises solemnly, "We will continue our investigation from the Frontline."

Continue they may have, but without reportable results. However, more than a few *Frontline* programs have had a discernible influence upon the subjects of their stories: "Hot Guns" (1997) caused California State Assembly member Jack Scott to author the Firearms Manufacturer Accountability Act designed to curb the black market sale of firearms;

"A Class Divided" (1985/86/95) has become an important element of diversity training in schools and other institutions throughout the country; "Waco—The Inside Story" (1995/96) is used by the FBI for hostage situation training; and "Global Dumping Ground" (1990) prompted a UN resolution calling for a ban on developed countries' dumping toxic waste in the third world.

The *Fort Lauderdale News and Sun Sentinel* called the NFL program an "explosive documentary" (a description appearing in many newspapers), adding, "This is not a documentary that NBC or CBS or ABC, which all televise the NFL, could have made." David Klein, writing in *The Cincinnati Post,* predicted that if the series kept this up it would soon be in hot water with some powerful people, and that "this is just as it should be."

Reviewers seemed somewhat startled that the program had been produced by public television. It was described favorably, as have most subsequent programs in the series. "If *Frontline* sustains the controversy and drama packed into the first program," wrote the *Kansas City Star's* Gerald Jordan, "it should bring honors and horrors to PBS." Both were sustained in the 1983 season: the NFL program was followed by reports on adoption, gun control, abortion, Taiwan, the Vatican's bank, and a program describing poverty in Washington, D.C. (timed to coincide with Reagan's State of the Union address).

"I seem to remember that the second season was much more cautious than the first," Fanning has reflected. "I can only think that it was an entirely human reaction to a fair amount of stuff that got stirred up . . . just the existence of Jessica and assorted problems . . ."

About every three years, he says, he feels a need to "reinvent" the series, based, in part, upon where the culture is going. "We're out of the Cold War and turning inwards, looking at the world differently. You have to keep trying to replenish. There are certain sorts of programs that will get you ratings: you can go after Mafiosi, certain kinds of crime stories. You can certainly do sex crimes. But we always end up trying to find that place that asks the unexpected, the harder questions." This, of course, means seeking new producers with fresh ideas.

"The hard thing to have to admit," he says, "is that there aren't that many people out there who know how to do this craft."

Going into its fifth season, *Frontline* was television's highest-rated public affairs series on PBS with 7.2 million viewers each week. It had produced five of the ten highest-rated PBS programs. Judy Woodruff, a former White House correspondent who had appeared briefly on the *MacNeil/Lehrer NewsHour,* replaced Jessica Savitch. Broadcasting awards, including a Peabody and eleven Emmys, showered down. In four years *Frontline* had employed nearly forty independent producers who had created one hundred programs. By 1988 Fanning had produced 170 programs broadcast on PBS. A one million dollar budget increase in that year added time that producers could spend in the field and in the editing room, something that, as Fanning remarked, "could make the difference between a good film and a great film." *Frontline* was now consistently matching the viewership of the popular *Masterpiece Theatre, Mystery,* and *American Playhouse.*

As the series approached its tenth season, one that saw twenty-seven new programs, productions continued to be driven more by stories than topics and Fanning continued to look, according to writer B.J. Bullert, "for filmmakers who combine journalistic curiosity and discipline with authorial literary skill . . ." After a decade, *Frontline* had begun to settle comfortably into a list of distinguished documentary series that included Murrow and Friendly's *See It Now* (CBS, begun in 1951), *CBS Reports* (1959), the Huntley-Brinkley *NBC White Papers* (1960), and CBS's *60 Minutes.* Hodding Carter, author and sometimes TV producer, said, "There has to be some underlying envy of a relatively small news outfit that can without visible strain give you a rich portrait of the Amazon rain forest one week and state lottery operations the next—and find the deeper meanings behind both."

As *Frontline* continues to present more than two dozen programs each year there are few dimensions of American political, economic, and social life it has neglected to explore: "My Doctor, My Lover" (1991); "The Kevorkian File" (1994); "Murder on Abortion Row" (1996); "Behind the Mask: The IRA and Sinn Fein" (1997). Titles like these reflect an extraordinary range of investigative reporting. Fanning says he "flinches slightly" at this description. "You investigate values as much as you investigate whistle blowers and wrongdoing. . . . That's the task of this series." Few programs have aroused the strenuous response of "Death of a Princess," but some, such as "L.A. is Burning: Five Reports from a Divided City" (1993), have come close. Fanning's praise for the support he has received from WGBH during so many seasons of controversial productions is unstinting: "I have never had anybody intervene. I have never in my entire career at WGBH had anybody above me come into an editing room or after a screening or with a finished film in hand and say, 'I want you to change this.' I don't believe there's another television station in the world that you could say that about with a series of this import and weight in a weekly series for fifteen years. I think that's staggering."

Perhaps inevitably there are misgivings as one season follows another. In this Fanning is not unlike other producers who have seen their series become part of the PBS "core schedule," a central ingredient of what public television contributes to America's cultural life: "I don't think we've always done a good job. We've made some weak films. We've missed some opportunities. We've been a little arrogant . . . diffuse at times, and self-indulgent. We've let films go too long, allowed producers to be indulgent. In my low moments I feel some real failure about that . . . and ask myself whether I [don't] just need to get the hell out. [Still], it's hard for me to separate out my own personal selfish desire to keep being around, because it's the last best place on television."

I am indebted to Michael Ambrosino, former executive producer of *NOVA* and sometime *Frontline* producer, for allowing me to use the transcript of his lengthy 1997 interview with David Fanning, from which most of the quotes from Fanning have been drawn.

Index

About the Author

DAVID STEWART has been a public television program executive for more than forty years, and has produced public television documentaries in Washington, D.C., for the Library of Congress, the National Gallery of Art, the Smithsonian, the Folger Shakespeare Library, and major universities. As the first director of film, TV, and radio for the National Endowment for the Arts, he established the American Film Institute. He joined the Corporation for Public Broadcasting when it was created and for nearly twenty years was its director of international activities. He holds degrees from Case-Western Reserve University and Columbia University and has taught dramatic literature at Vassar College, Case-Western, and Robert College in Istanbul (where he established a theater). In addition to articles ranging from the arts and media to archeology appearing in scholarly journals, he has written numerous articles for popular magazines, one of which (on Renoir's "The Luncheon of the Boating Party") won an art/journalism award. He lives in Washington, D.C., where he is a contributing editor of *Current Newspaper.*